Busy Ant Maths

Assessment Guide 1

Series editor: Peter Clarke

William Collins' dream of knowledge for all began with the publication of his first book in 1819.
A self-educated mill worker, he not only enriched millions of lives, but also founded a flourishing publishing house. Today, staying true to this spirit, Collins books are packed with inspiration, innovation and practical expertise. They place you at the centre of a world of possibility and give you exactly what you need to explore it.

Collins. Freedom to teach.

Published by Collins

An imprint of HarperCollinsPublishers
1 London Bridge Street
London
SE1 9GF

Browse the complete Collins catalogue at
www.collins.co.uk

© HarperCollins*Publishers* Limited 2014

10 9 8 7 6 5 4 3 2 1

ISBN 978-0-00-756815-4

Peter Clarke and Steven Matchett assert their moral rights to be identified as the authors of this work.

British Library Cataloguing in Publication Data
A Catalogue record for this publication is available from the British Library

Commissioned by Fiona McGlade
Managing editor Caroline Green
Project editor Amanda Redstone
Edited by Tanya Solomons and Marie Taylor
Proofread by Laura Booth
Cover design and artwork by Amparo Barrera
Internal design and typesetting by Ken Vail Graphic Design
Illustrations by Ken Vail Graphic Design and Louise Forshaw
Production by Robin Forrester

Printed and bound by Martins the Printer, Berwick upon Tweed

Contents

End-of-unit Tests

Pupil Self-assessments

Record-keeping formats

Resources to accompany the Assessment Tasks

Tracking back and forward through the Mathematics National Curriculum attainment targets – Year 1

Introduction

Assessment Tasks and Exercises

Domain		National Curriculum attainment target	Assessment Task / Exercise
Number –	Number and place value	Count to and across 100, forwards and backwards, beginning with 0 or 1, or from any given number	1
		Count, read and write numbers to 100 in numerals; count in multiples of twos, fives and tens	2
		Given a number, identify one more and one less	3
		Identify and represent numbers using objects and pictorial representations including the number line, and use the language of: equal to, more than, less than (fewer), most, least	4
		Read and write numbers from 1 to 20 in numerals and words	5
Number –	Addition and subtraction	Read, write and interpret mathematical statements involving addition (+), subtraction (−) and equals (=) signs	6
		Represent and use number bonds and related subtraction facts within 20	7
		Add and subtract one-digit and two-digit numbers to 20, including zero	8
		Solve one-step problems that involve addition and subtraction, using concrete objects and pictorial representations, and missing number problems such as $7 = \square - 9$	9
Number –	Multiplication and division	Solve one-step problems involving multiplication and division, by calculating the answer using concrete objects, pictorial representations and arrays with the support of the teacher	10
Number –	Fractions	Recognise, find and name a half as one of two equal parts of an object, shape or quantity	11
		Recognise, find and name a quarter as one of four equal parts of an object, shape or quantity	12

Domain	National Curriculum attainment target	Assessment Task / Exercise

Measurement	Compare, describe and solve practical problems for:
	  – lengths and heights [for example, long/short, longer/shorter, tall/short, double/half]
	  – mass/weight [for example, heavy/light, heavier than, lighter than]
	  – capacity and volume [for example, full/empty, more than, less than, half, half full, quarter]
	  – time [for example, quicker, slower, earlier, later]
		13

	Measure and begin to record the following:
	  – lengths and heights
	  – mass/weight
	  – capacity and volume
	  – time (hours, minutes, seconds)
		14

	Recognise and know the value of different denominations of coins and notes	15
	Sequence events in chronological order using language [for example, before and after, next, first, today, yesterday, tomorrow, morning, afternoon and evening]	16
	Recognise and use language relating to dates, including days of the week, weeks, months and years	17
	Tell the time to the hour and half past the hour and draw the hands on a clock face to show these times	18

Geometry – Properties of shapes	Recognise and name common 2-D and 3-D shapes, including:
	  – 2-D shapes [for example, rectangles (including squares), circles and triangles]
	  – 3-D shapes [for example, cuboids (including cubes), pyramids and spheres]
		19

Geometry – Position and direction	Describe position, direction and movement, including whole, half, quarter and three-quarter turns	20

Key Principles of Busy Ant Maths Assessment

Busy Ant Maths identifies two main purposes of assessment:

• assessment *for* learning (ongoing formative assessment)

• assessment *of* learning (summative assessment).

Assessment *for* learning involves both pupils and teachers finding out about the specific strengths and weaknesses of individual pupils, and the class as a whole, and using this to inform future teaching and learning.

Assessment *for* learning:

– is part of the planning process

– is informed by learning objectives

– engages pupils in the assessment process

– recognises the achievements of *all* pupils

– takes account of how pupils learn

– motivates learners.

Assessment *of* learning is any assessment that summarises at what level individual pupils, and the class as a whole, are working at a given point in time. It provides a snapshot of what has been learned.

The Busy Ant Maths Assessment Guides provide guidance in both assessment *for* learning and assessment *of* learning.

The Busy Ant Maths Assessment Guides consist of seven key components:

• Assessment Tasks

• Assessment Exercises

• End-of-unit Tests

• Pupil Self-assessments

• Record-keeping formats

• Resources to accompany the Assessment Tasks

• Tracking back and forward through the Mathematics National Curriculum attainment targets – Year 1.

The contents of the Assessment Guide is available in Word and PDF formats on our online learning platform, Collins Connect. Collins Connect also contains a powerful record-keeping tool which can be used to record results and teacher judgements, as well as track the progress and attainment of pupils throughout a year, between year groups and across a Key Stage. Assessment data can be stored online and presented digitally for class and whole-school analysis.

Introduction

Assessment, record-keeping and reporting continue the teaching and learning cycle and are used to form the basis of adjustments to the teaching programme.

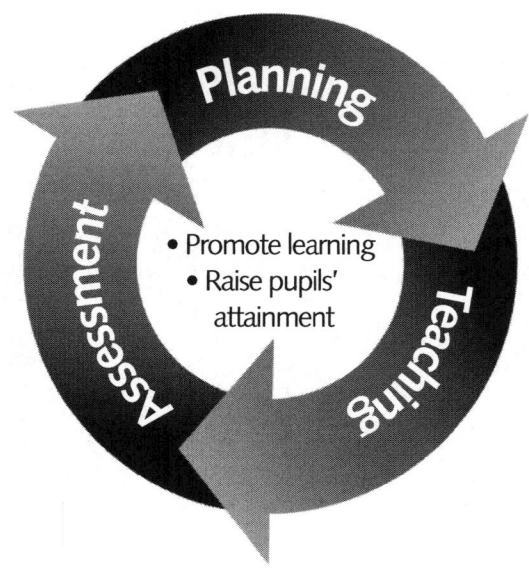

Busy Ant Maths offers manageable and meaningful assessment on four levels:

- **Diagnostic assessment**

   The Assessment Tasks are designed to assist teachers in determining pupils' readiness for a particular Busy Ant Maths unit of work. They are designed to yield information that will directly support individual pupils and whole-class teaching.

- **Short-term 'ongoing' assessment**

   Progress Check Questions ▶ are an important feature of every Busy Ant Maths lesson and are linked to specific learning objectives. They are designed to provide immediate feedback to pupils and to gauge pupil progress in order to adapt teaching.

   Shared Success criteria are also provided in each lesson to assist pupils in identifying the steps required to achieve mastery of the learning objective.

- **Medium-term 'formative' assessment**

   As well as being used for diagnostic assessment, the Assessment Tasks, along with the Assessment Exercises, can be used to review and record the progress of both individual pupils and the class as a whole, in relation to the National Curriculum attainment targets.

   An End-of-unit Test is provided for each of the 12 Busy Ant Maths units. Each test is designed to assess the mathematics covered during the three-week unit.

   The formative Assessment Tasks, Exercises and Tests provide individual and/or group opportunities to identify those pupils who have not yet achieved (NYA), or who have achieved and exceeded (A&E) national expectations. They can also be used to set individual targets for pupils.

- **Long-term 'summative' assessment**

   The various record-keeping formats found in this Assessment Guide and on Collins Connect are designed to show individual pupils' level of mastery against national standards. They draw on the data gathered throughout the year, including results from Assessment Tasks, Exercises and Tests, performance in whole-class discussions, participation in group work, written evidence and any other supplementary notes. It is these documents that form the basis for reporting to parents and guardians and informing the next year's teacher. Importantly, they also help to identify whether pupils are on track to meet end of key stage expectations.

Assessment Tasks

Purposes

- To assess individual pupils' level of mastery in a specific National Curriculum attainment target (NC AT).

- To identify individual pupils' strengths and weaknesses in a specific NC AT.

- To provide guidance about what to do for those pupils who are achieving *above* or *below* expectations.

- To inform future planning and teaching of individual pupils and the class as a whole.

When to use the Assessment Tasks

When teachers are uncertain about a pupil's, or group of pupils', level of mastery in a specific NC AT, the Assessment Tasks can be used as diagnostic tools either:

- at the start of a new unit, or

- at any other time throughout the year.

How to use the Assessment Tasks

- An Assessment Task is used in conjunction with the *Assessment Task Record* (see page 11). There are two versions of the *Assessment Task Record*: a paper version (see page 71) and an electronic, pre-populated version found on Collins Connect and accessed via computer or tablet.

- If using the paper version of the *Assessment Task Record*:

  - photocopy page 71 and complete the top section

  - write the names of the pupils you are assessing (there is sufficient space for up to four pupils)

  - copy the Success criteria from the relevant Assessment Task (there is sufficient space for up to six criteria (A–F). Only complete the number of rows required for the particular task you are undertaking.

- If using the electronic version of the *Assessment Task Record* on Collins Connect:

  - locate the relevant *Assessment Task Record*

  - complete the top section

  - add the names of the pupils you are assessing.

- Use the *Assessment Task Record* to record each pupil's performance during the task, indicating how competent a pupil is in each of the Success criteria, commenting on particular strengths and weaknesses. If necessary, make a note of any additional considerations observed. Once the pupils have completed the task, make a judgement of each pupil's mastery of the NC AT by highlighting whether the pupil has 'Not yet achieved' (NYA), 'Achieved' (A) or 'Achieved and exceeded' (A&E). Also make a note of any future action that may be considered appropriate. Refer to page 11 for a more detailed explanation of how to use the *Assessment Task Record*.

Introduction

- If using the paper version, transfer the information collected on the *Assessment Task Record* onto the *Whole-class National Curriculum Attainment Targets* record (see pages 18 and 19) and the pupil's *Individual Pupil National Curriculum Attainment Targets and Domains* record (see page 22).

- If using the electronic version of the *Assessment Task Record*, you can populate the data in the record-keeping tool. This data can be presented digitally as per the *Whole-class National Curriculum Attainment Targets* record (see pages 18 and 19) and the pupil's *Individual Pupil National Curriculum Attainment Targets and Domains* record (see page 22).

❶ Assessment Task number

In most cases the numbering of the Assessment Tasks corresponds with the numbering of the Assessment Exercises.

❷ National Curriculum Programme of Study Domain

❸ National Curriculum attainment target (NC AT)

❹ Prerequisite checklist

List of the prerequisite knowledge, skills and understanding pupils need to have in order to achieve mastery of the NC AT.

❺ Success criteria

A list of the Success criteria that pupils need to know, understand and do in order to demonstrate that they have achieved mastery of the NC AT.

❻ Resources

List of resources required to undertake the task, including reference to any resource sheets.

❼ Assessment Task

Description of the task including 'What to do', 'What to say' and 'What to look for'.

❽ What to do for those pupils working *below* or *above* expectations

If a pupil has Not yet achieved (NYA) mastery or has Achieved and exceeded (A&E) mastery, the ❾'Tracking back and forward through the Mathematics National Curriculum attainment targets' charts on pages 193–200 will help to determine at what year group the pupil is currently working. Related Assessment Tasks and Assessment Exercises can then be located in the corresponding Busy Ant Maths Assessment Guide. Related teaching and learning opportunities can be found in the corresponding Busy Ant Maths Teacher's Guide.

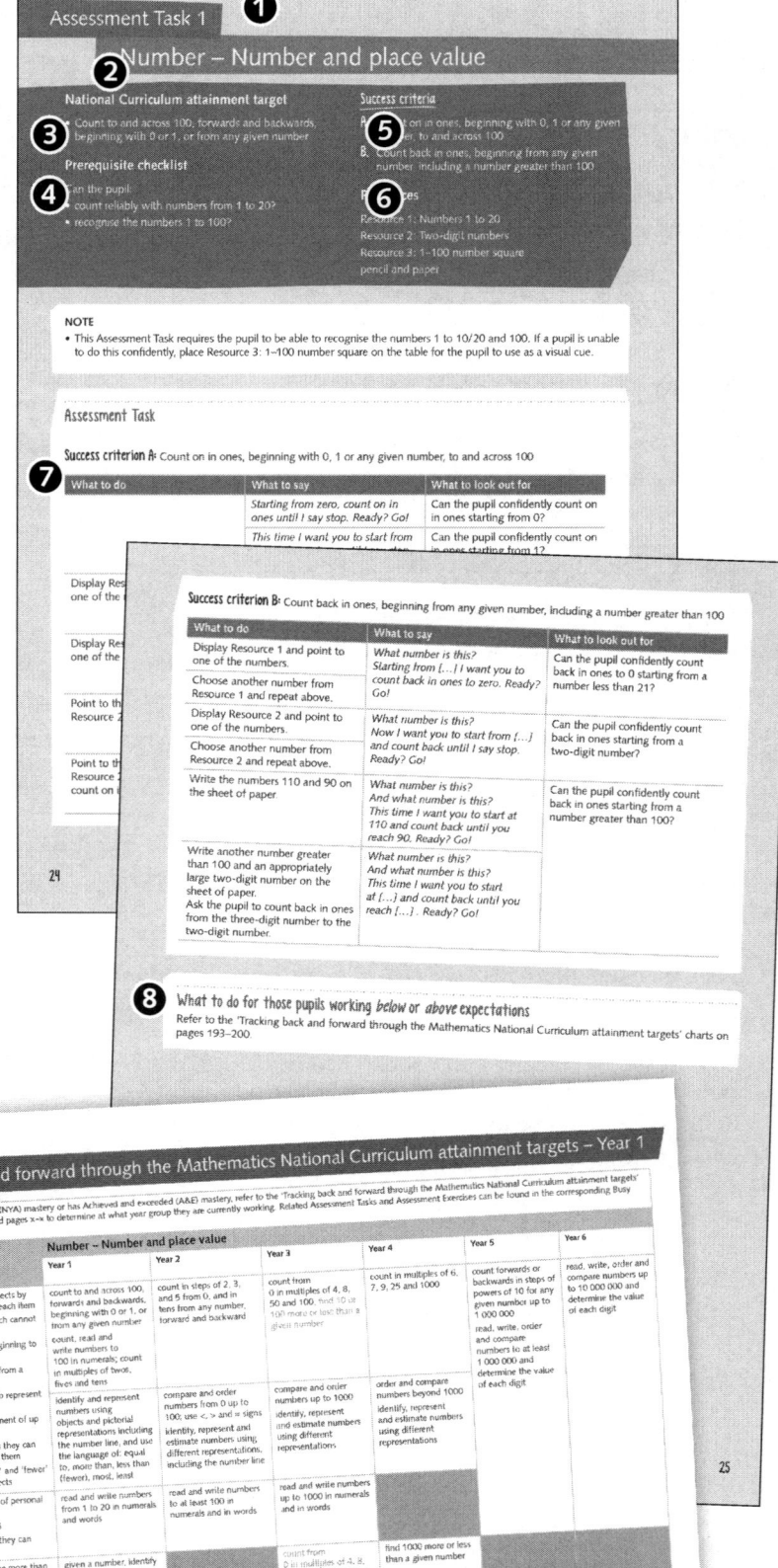

Assessment Task Record

The Assessment Task Record is used in conjunction with the Assessment Tasks (see pages 9 and 10).

❶ National Curriculum Programme of Study Domain
Copy this information from the relevant Assessment Task.

❷ National Curriculum attainment target (NC AT)
Copy this information from the relevant Assessment Task.

❸ Teacher, class and date reference

❹ Pupils' names
Write the names of the pupils you are assessing (there is sufficient space for up to four pupils).

❺ Success criteria
The Success criteria for the relevant task are written in the spaces provided. There is sufficient space for up to six criteria (A–F). Only complete the number of rows required for the particular task you are undertaking. As you assess each pupil against the different Success criteria, either make a written comment on their level of mastery or use the following abbreviations: NYA (Not yet achieved), A (Achieved) or A&E (Achieved and exceeded).

❻ Other observations
For commenting on particular strengths or weaknesses or any other relevant observations made while undertaking the task with the pupil.

❼ Level of mastery of NC AT
The degree to which a pupil has mastered the specific NC AT is shown by ticking one of the following boxes:
NYA – Not yet achieved
A – Achieved
A&E – Achieved and exceeded

❽ Future action
Notes on any future action that may be considered appropriate.

BUSY ANT MATHS | Assessment Guide 1 | Assessment Task Record

❶ Domain: _____

❷ National Curriculum attainment target (NC AT): _____

❸ Teacher: _____ Class: _____ Date: _____

❺ Success criteria	❹ Name			
A				
B				
C				
D				
E				
F				
❻ Other observations				
❼ Level of mastery of NC AT*	NYA A A&E	NYA A A&E	NYA A A&E	NYA A A&E
❽ Future action				

Level of mastery key: NYA – Not yet achieved I A – Achieved I A&E – Achieved and exceeded

Assessment Exercises

Purposes

- To assess individual pupils' level of mastery in a specific National Curriculum attainment target (NC AT).

- To identify individual pupils' strengths and weaknesses in a specific NC AT.

- To identify those pupils who are achieving *above* or *below* expectations.

- To inform future planning and teaching of individual pupils and the class as a whole.

When to use the Assessment Exercises

- Any time throughout the year when teachers are uncertain about a pupil's, or group of pupils', level of mastery in a specific NC AT.

- When requiring written evidence of a pupil's level of mastery in a specific NC AT.

- Assessment Exercises differ from the End-of-unit Tests (see pages 14 and 15) in that an Assessment Exercise is designed to assess mastery in a specific NC AT, i.e. the *end-of-year level of expectation,* whereas an End-of-unit Test assesses all of the NC ATs taught in a particular Busy Ant Maths unit. It is designed to assess the exact mathematical content that has been taught during the unit and therefore will not always assess *the end-of-year level of expectation*.

How to use the Assessment Exercises

- This section provides a photocopiable pupil Assessment Exercise and accompanying teacher's notes with answers and marking commentary for each of the NC ATs.

- The way in which the Assessment Exercises are administered is entirely up to the discretion of the individual teacher.

- It is advised that before pupils begin an exercise, you read through and explain the exercise to the pupils to ensure that they understand each of the questions. Also ensure that pupils have any necessary resources.

- After marking the Assessment Exercise, you then decide, based on the results of the exercise, the level of mastery achieved by the pupil for that specific NC AT, i.e. 'Not yet achieved' (NYA), 'Achieved' (A) or 'Achieved and exceeded' (A&E).

- The data collected can then be used to update either the paper or electronic versions of the *Whole-class National Curriculum Attainment Targets* record (see pages 18 and 19) and the pupil's *Individual Pupil National Curriculum Attainment Targets and Domains* record (see page 22).

❶ Assessment Exercise number

In most cases the numbering of the Assessment Exercises corresponds with the numbering of the Assessment Tasks.

❷ National Curriculum Programme of Study Domain

❸ National Curriculum attainment target (NC AT)

❹ Marking scheme

❺ Results panel

This includes the pupil's score and the level of mastery achieved.

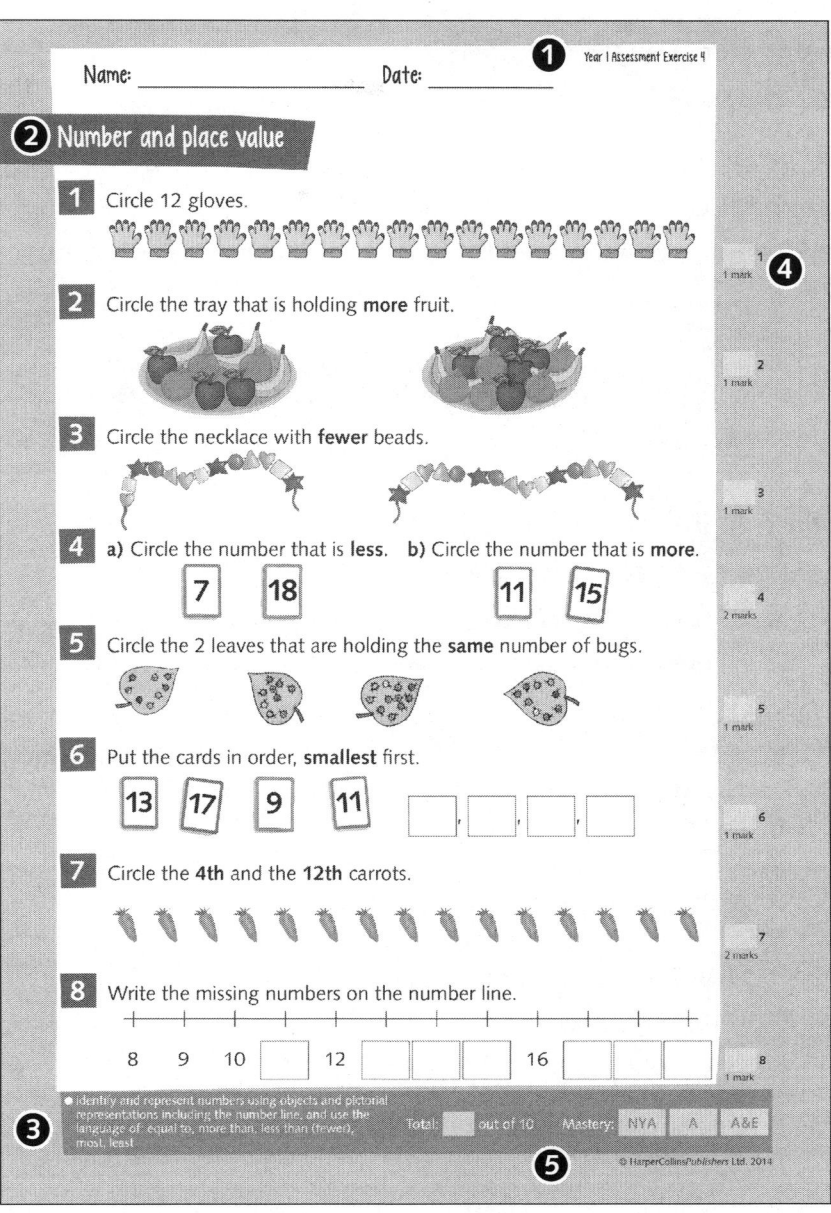

❻ Oral questions
(where required)

❼ Answers

❽ Marking commentary

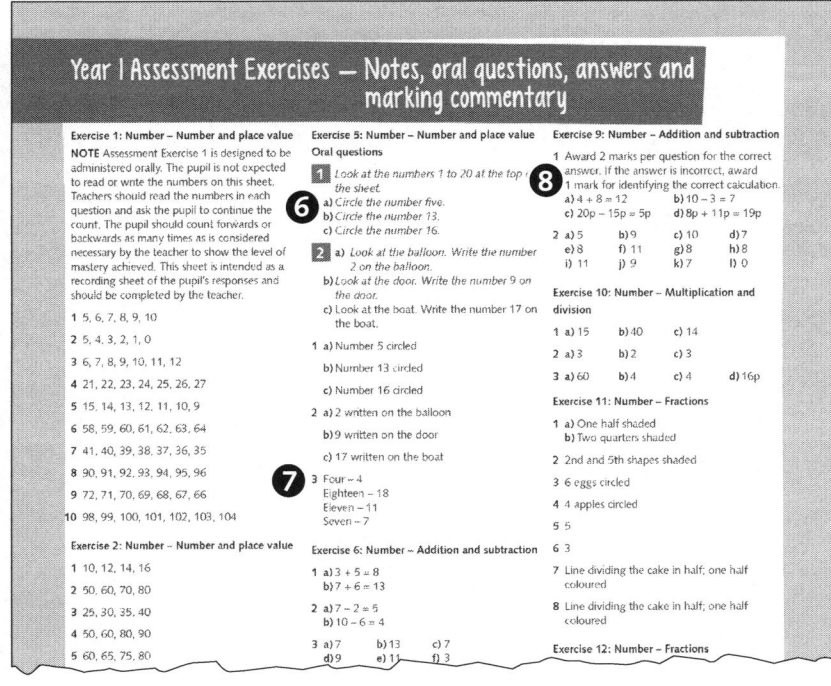

End-of-unit Tests

Purposes

- To assess understanding of the concepts taught in a Busy Ant Maths unit.

- To assist teachers in assessing individual pupils' level of mastery in a particular National Curriculum Programme of Study Domain.

- To inform future planning and teaching of individual pupils and the class as a whole.

- To identify those pupils who are achieving *above* or *below* expectations.

When to use the End-of-unit Tests

- At the end of a three-week Busy Ant Maths unit.

- Alternatively, as each End-of-unit Test consists of three pages – one page per week, a page (test) could be used at the end of each week. However, this use of the End-of-unit Tests is not recommended as it could result in Friday becoming 'maths test day'.

- End-of-unit Tests differ from the Assessment Exercises (see pages 12 and 13) in that an End-of-unit Test assesses all of the National Curriculum attainment targets (NC ATs) taught in a particular Busy Ant Maths unit. They are designed to assess the exact mathematical content that has been taught during the unit and therefore will not always assess *the end-of-year level of expectation*. An Assessment Exercise, however, is designed to assess mastery in a specific NC AT, i.e. the *end-of-year level of expectation*.

How to use the End-of-unit Tests

- This section provides a three-page photocopiable test, and accompanying teacher's notes with answers and marking commentary, for each of the 12 Busy Ant Maths units. End-of-unit Tests consist of one page of questions per week taught within that unit, assessing the NC ATs taught during that week.

- The way that the End-of-unit Tests are administered is entirely up to the discretion of the individual teacher.

- It is advised that before pupils begin a test, you read through and explain the test to the pupils to ensure that they understand each of the questions. Also ensure that pupils have any necessary resources.

- After marking each page of an End-of-unit Test, you then decide, based on the results of the page, the level of mastery achieved by the pupil for that particular Domain, i.e. 'Not yet achieved' (NYA), 'Achieved' (A) or 'Achieved and exceeded' (A&E).

- The data collected can then be used to update either the paper or electronic version of the *Whole-class National Curriculum Attainment Targets* record (see pages 18 and 19), the *Whole-class Domains* record (see pages 20 and 21) and the pupil's *Individual Pupil National Curriculum Attainment Targets and Domains* record (see page 22).

❶ Marking scheme

❷ Teacher reference and results panel
This includes year group, Busy Ant Maths unit number and week, National Curriculum Programme of Study Domain and the pupil's score and level of mastery achieved.

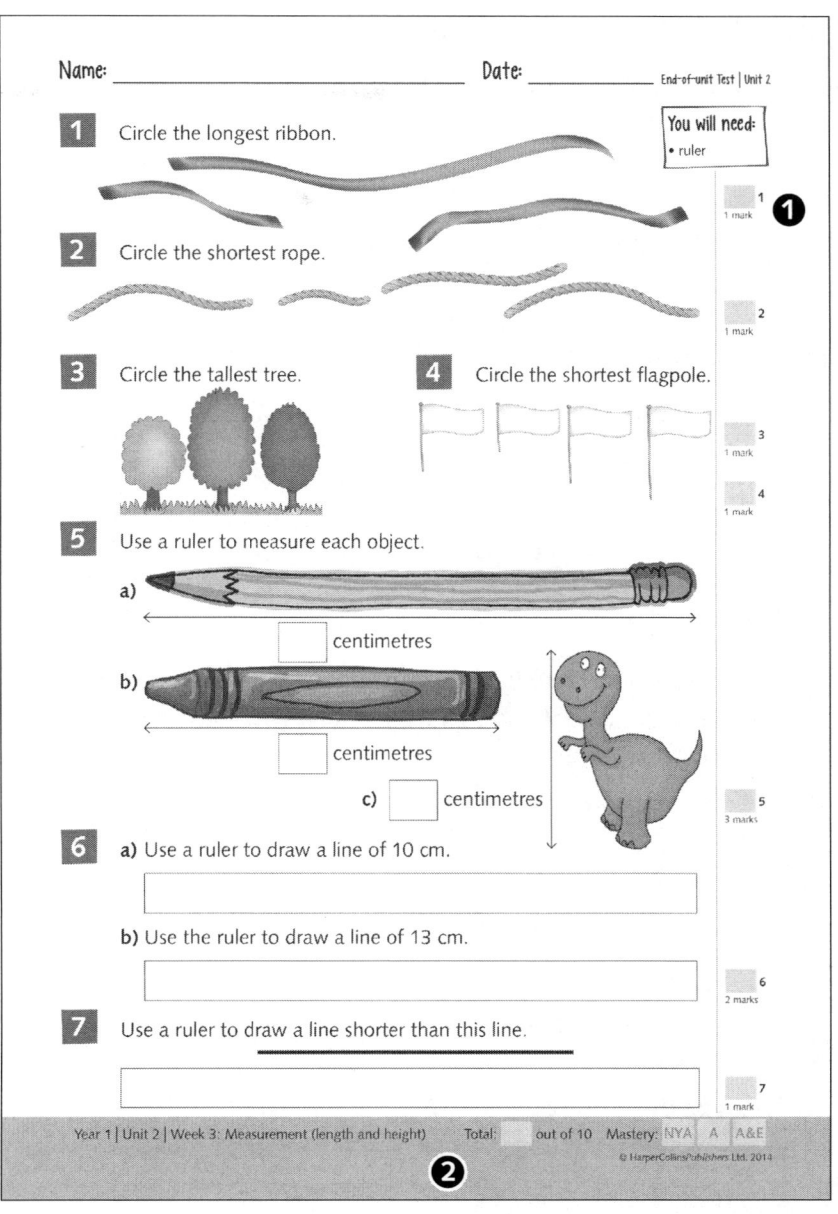

❸ Answers

❹ Marking commentary

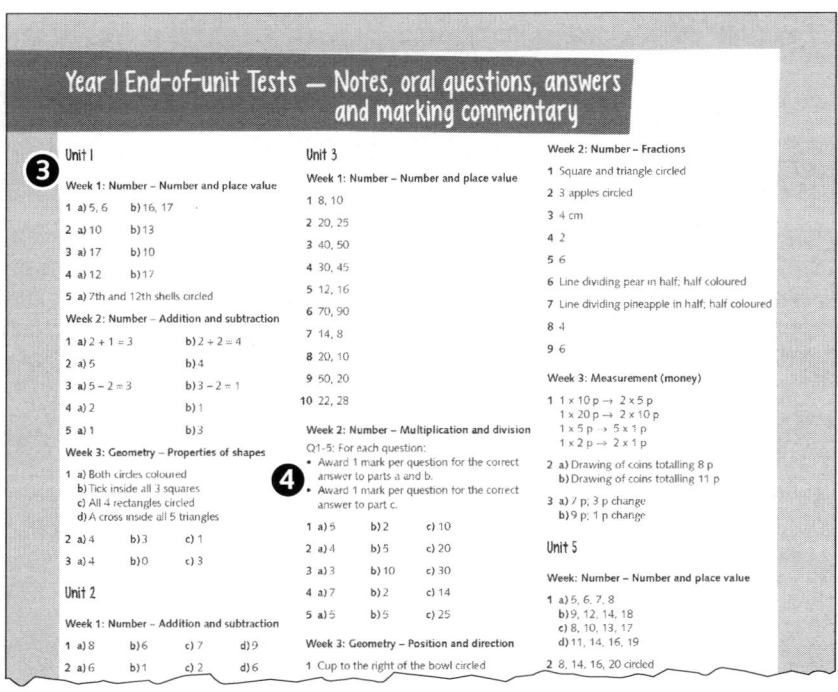

Pupil Self-assessments

Purpose

- To provide pupils with the opportunity to undertake some form of self-assessment at the end of a Busy Ant Maths unit.

When and how to use the Pupil Self-assessments

Either:

1. Distribute the relevant Pupil Self-assessment at the *start of each week*. Pupils make a judgement about their current level of understanding for each of the 'I can' statements for the week. At the end of each week pupils revisit the booklet to re-assess their level of understanding.

   or

2. Distribute the relevant Pupil Self-assessment at the *end of the unit*. Pupils think back to the start of the unit and make a judgement about their level of understanding for each of the 'I can' statements for each week. At the same time they also make a judgement about their current level of understanding now that the unit has been taught.

- The empty box at the bottom of each page is designed to be used by pupils to record anything special that you may like them to have a record of, for example:
  - a relevant piece of work, drawing, calculation, statement or other piece of written evidence
  - anything the pupil feels they need more practice on
  - what the pupil thinks they should or could learn next
  - any special equipment that the pupil used to help them during the unit
  - anything the pupil particularly liked or disliked that they did during the unit.

- After pupils have completed a page (or the entire booklet) as a class, discuss specific statements, asking individual pupils to comment on what they have written.

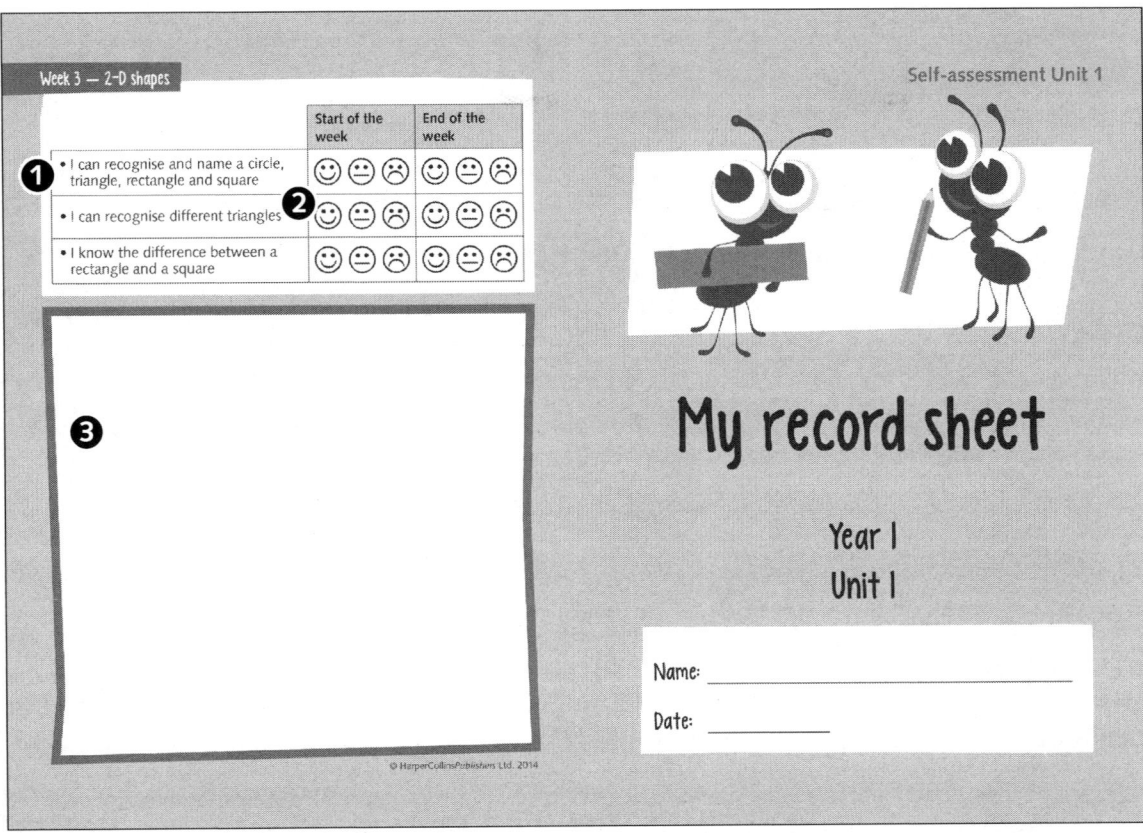

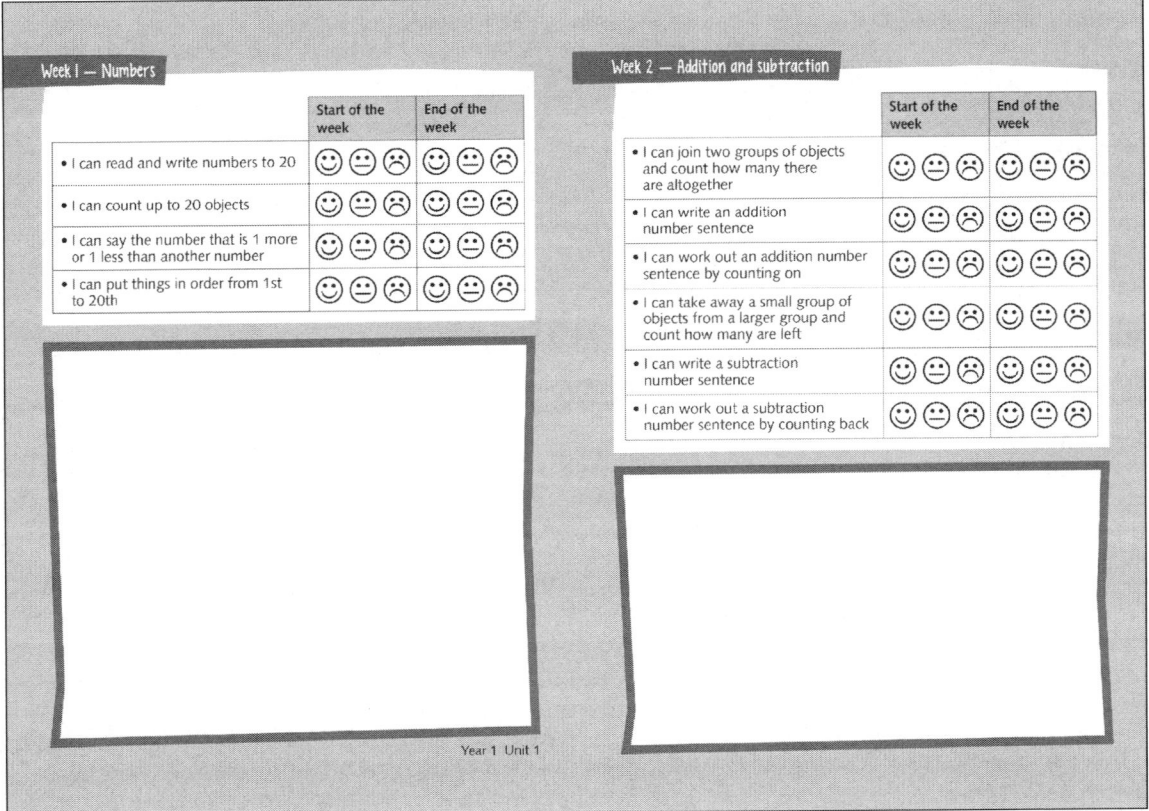

❶ List of assessment criteria in pupil-friendly language

❷ Icons for the pupil's self-assessment, both at the start and end of each week

❸ Box for the pupil to record something the teacher wants them to have a record of

Record-keeping formats

There are three different types of record-keeping format in each of the Busy Ant Maths Assessment Guides:

- *Whole-class National Curriculum Attainment Targets* (see pages 157 to 163).

- *Whole-class Domains* (two versions: Views 1 and 2 – schools should choose their preferred version) (see pages 164 and 165).

- *Individual Pupil National Curriculum Attainment Targets and Domains* (see pages 166 and 167).

 Each of these formats is available as a paper version to photocopy and complete, and in electronic format on Collins Connect.

To ensure that pupils' attainment within a year group, and progression across the year groups, is easy to track, the same formats have been used throughout the entire Busy Ant Maths course.

Whole-class National Curriculum attainment targets

This record-keeping format is designed to record the level of mastery that all the pupils in the class have achieved in each of the National Curriculum attainment targets (NC AT). Decisions as to an individual pupil's level of mastery in each of the NC ATs should take into account:

- performance in whole-class discussions
- participation in group work
- work presented in exercise books
- observations made during Assessment Tasks
- performance in the Assessment Exercises or End-of-unit Tests
- any other evidence.

As a result of the evidence collected for each NC AT, you can then make a judgement regarding the overall level of mastery in each of the National Curriculum Programme of Study Domains.

This record-keeping format is intended to be a working document that teachers start to complete at the beginning of the academic year that can be continually updated and amended throughout the course of the year.

At the end of the year, this document will help teachers when reporting to parents. It will also help senior managers with data analysis and assist in informing the next year's teacher of those pupils who are working *above* and *below* national expectations in each of the NC ATs and Domains.

Using the *Whole-class National Curriculum Attainment Targets* record-keeping format:

- When a judgement concerning a specific NC AT is made on the *Whole-class National Curriculum Attainment Targets* record, this data should then be updated on the pupil's *Individual Pupil National Curriculum Attainment Targets and Domains* record.

- When a judgement concerning the overall level of mastery in a particular Domain is made on the *Whole-class National Curriculum Attainment Targets* record, this data should then be updated on the pupil's *Individual Pupil National Curriculum Attainment Targets and Domains* record and either version of the *Whole-class Domains* record.

❶ Year group

❷ Class and academic year reference

❸ National Curriculum Programme of Study Domain

❹ Pupils' names

❺ National Curriculum attainment targets (NC AT)

❻ Level of mastery in each NC AT

The degree to which a pupil has mastered a NC AT is shown by writing one of the following initials or sets of initials in the appropriate column:

NYA – Not yet achieved

A – Achieved

A&E – Achieved and exceeded

❼ Overall level of mastery for this National Curriculum Programme of Study Domain

The degree to which a pupil has mastered the Domain is shown by writing one of the following initials or sets of initials in the appropriate column:

NYA – Not yet achieved

A – Achieved

A&E – Achieved and exceeded

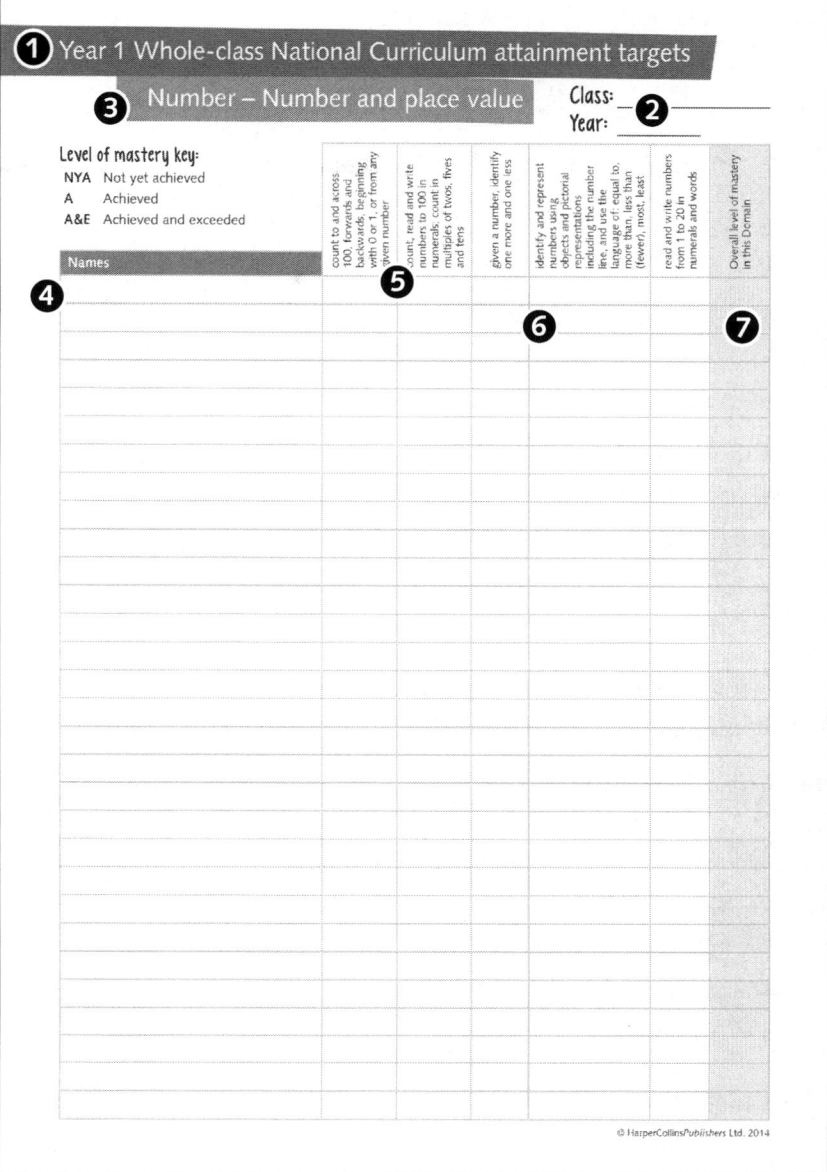

❶ Year 1 Whole-class National Curriculum attainment targets

❸ Number – Number and place value

Class: **❷**

Year:

Level of mastery key:

NYA   Not yet achieved

A   Achieved

A&E   Achieved and exceeded

© HarperCollinsPublishers Ltd. 2014

Whole-class Domains Views 1 and 2

There are two record-keeping formats designed to record the level of mastery that all the pupils in the class have achieved in each of the National Curriculum Programme of Study Domains. These are:

– *Whole-class Domains* (View 1)

– *Whole-class Domains* (View 2).

Schools should decide which version they prefer and just use *one* of these record-keeping formats.

Decisions as to an individual pupil's level of mastery in each of the National Curriculum Programme of Study Domains should be based on each of the Domain's Attainment Targets and take into account:

– performance in whole class discussions

– participation in group work

– work presented in exercise books

– observations made during Assessment Tasks

– performance in the Assessment Exercises or End-of-unit Tests

– any other evidence.

This record-keeping format is intended to be a working document that teachers start to complete at the beginning of the academic year that can be continually updated and amended throughout the course of the year.

At the end of the year, this document will help teachers when reporting to parents. It will also help senior managers with data analysis and assist in informing the next year's teacher of those pupils who are working *above* and *below* national expectations in each of the National Curriculum Programme of Study Domains.

As with the other record-keeping formats, this format is available as a paper version to photocopy and complete, as well as in electronic format on Collins Connect.

Using the *Whole-class Domains* record-keeping format:

– When a judgement concerning the overall level of mastery in a particular Domain is made on either version of the *Whole-class Domains* records, this data should then be updated on a pupil's *Individual Pupil Attainment Targets and Domains* record and in the Domain column of the *Whole-class National Curriculum Attainment Targets* record.

Whole-class Domains (View 1)

❶ Year group

❷ Class and academic year reference

❸ National Curriculum Programme of Study Domains

❹ Pupils' names

❺ Overall level of mastery in the National Curriculum Programme of Study Domain

The degree of mastery achieved by a pupil in each Domain is shown by writing one of the following initials or sets of initials in the appropriate column:

NYA – Not yet achieved

A – Achieved

A&E – Achieved and exceeded

Whole-class Domains (View 2)

❶ Year group

❷ Class and academic year reference

❸ National Curriculum Programme of Study Domains

❹ National Curriculum attainment targets

❺ Overall level of mastery in the National Curriculum Programme of Study Domain

The degree of mastery achieved by a pupil in each Domain is shown by writing the pupil's name in the appropriate column:

NYA – Not yet achieved

A – Achieved

A&E – Achieved and exceeded

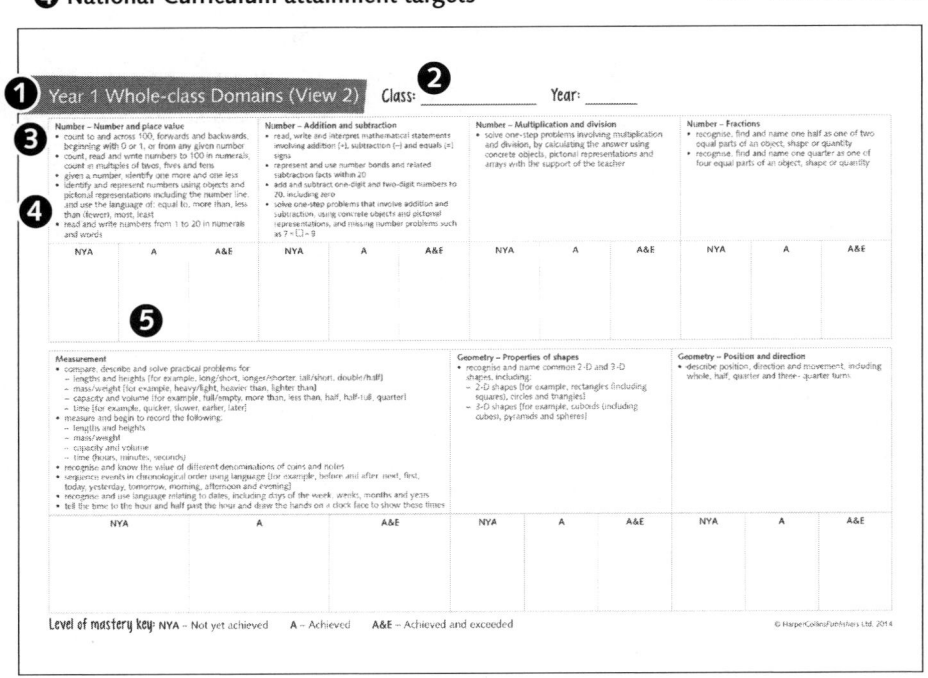

Individual Pupil National Curriculum Attainment Targets and Domains

This record-keeping format is designed to record individual pupils' level of mastery in each of the National Curriculum attainment targets (NC AT) and in each of the Programme of Study Domains, taking into account the following:

- – performance in whole-class discussions
- – participation in group work
- – work presented in exercise books
- – observations made during Assessment Tasks
- – performance in the Assessment Exercises or End-of-unit Tests
- – any other evidence.

This record-keeping format is intended to be a working document that teachers start to complete at the beginning of the academic year that can be continually updated and amended throughout the course of the year.

At the end of the year, this document will help teachers when reporting to parents. It will also help senior managers with data analysis and assist in informing the next year's teacher of those pupils who are working *above* and *below* national expectations in each of the NC ATs and Domains.

As with the other record-keeping formats, this format is available as a paper version to photocopy and complete, as well as in electronic format on Collins Connect.

Using the *Individual Pupil National Curriculum Attainment Targets and Domains* record-keeping format:

- – When a judgement about a pupil's level of mastery in a specific NC AT is made on the *Individual Pupil National Curriculum Attainment Targets and Domains* record, this data should then be updated on the *Whole-class National Curriculum Attainment Targets* record.

- – When a judgement concerning a pupil's overall level of mastery in a particular Domain is made on the *Individual Pupil National Curriculum Attainment Targets and Domains* record, this data should then be updated on the *Whole-class National Curriculum Attainment Targets* record and either version of the *Whole-class Domains* record.

❶ **Pupil's name**

❷ **Class and academic year reference**

❸ **National Curriculum Programme of Study Domain**

❹ **National Curriculum attainment target (NC AT)**

❺ **Level of mastery in each of the NC ATs**
The level of mastered achieved for each of the NC ATs is shown by ticking the appropriate column.

❻ **Overall level of mastery in each of the National Curriculum Programme of Study Domains**
The level of mastered achieved in each of the Domains is shown by ticking the appropriate column.

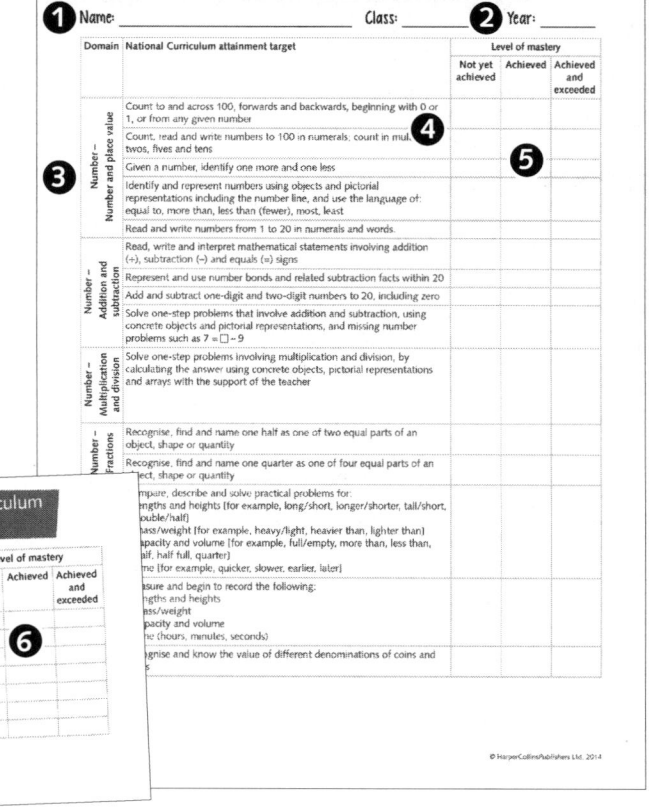

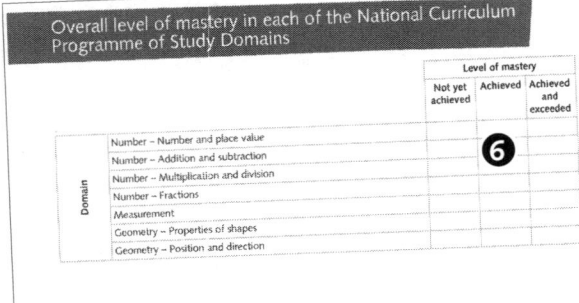

Resources to accompany the Assessment Tasks

This section includes all of the photocopiable resources that are required to administer each of the Assessment Tasks.

Number – Number and place value

National Curriculum attainment target

- Count to and across 100, forwards and backwards, beginning with 0 or 1, or from any given number

Prerequisite checklist

Can the pupil:
- count reliably with numbers from 1 to 20?
- recognise the numbers 1 to 100?

Success criteria

A. Count on in ones, beginning with 0, 1 or any given number, to and across 100

B. Count back in ones, beginning from any given number, including a number greater than 100

Resources

Resource 1: Numbers 1 to 20

Resource 2: Two-digit numbers

Resource 3: 1–100 number square

pencil and paper

NOTE

- This Assessment Task requires the pupil to be able to recognise the numbers 1 to 10/20 and 100. If a pupil is unable to do this confidently, place Resource 3: 1–100 number square on the table for the pupil to use as a visual cue.

Assessment Task

Success criterion A: Count on in ones, beginning with 0, 1 or any given number, to and across 100

What to do	What to say	What to look out for
	Starting from zero, count on in ones until I say stop. Ready? Go!	Can the pupil confidently count on in ones starting from 0?
	This time I want you to start from one and count on until I say stop. Ready? Go!	Can the pupil confidently count on in ones starting from 1?
Display Resource 1 and point to one of the numbers.	*What number is this? Now I want you to start from […] and count on until I say stop. Ready? Go!*	Can the pupil confidently count on in ones starting from a number less than 21?
Display Resource 2 and point to one of the numbers less than 80.	*What number is this? Now I want you to start from […] and count on until I say stop. Ready? Go!*	Can the pupil confidently count on in ones starting from a number less than 80?
Point to the number 86 on Resource 2.	*What number is this? This time I want you to start from 86 and count on until you reach 100. Ready? Go!*	Can the pupil confidently count on in ones to 100?
Point to the number 93 or 98 on Resource 2 and ask the pupil to count on in ones beyond 100.	*What number is this? This time I want you to start from […] and count on until I say stop. Ready? Go!*	Can the pupil confidently count on in ones beyond 100?

Success criterion B: Count back in ones, beginning from any given number, including a number greater than 100

What to do	What to say	What to look out for
Display Resource 1 and point to one of the numbers.	*What number is this?* *Starting from […] I want you to count back in ones to zero. Ready? Go!*	Can the pupil confidently count back in ones to 0 starting from a number less than 21?
Choose another number from Resource 1 and repeat above.		
Display Resource 2 and point to one of the numbers.	*What number is this?* *Now I want you to start from […] and count back until I say stop. Ready? Go!*	Can the pupil confidently count back in ones starting from a two-digit number?
Choose another number from Resource 2 and repeat above.		
Write the numbers 110 and 90 on the sheet of paper.	*What number is this?* *And what number is this?* *This time I want you to start at 110 and count back until you reach 90. Ready? Go!*	Can the pupil confidently count back in ones starting from a number greater than 100?
Write another number greater than 100 and an appropriately large two-digit number on the sheet of paper. Ask the pupil to count back in ones from the three-digit number to the two-digit number.	*What number is this?* *And what number is this?* *This time I want you to start at […] and count back until you reach […] . Ready? Go!*	

What to do for those pupils working *below* or *above* expectations

Refer to the 'Tracking back and forward through the Mathematics National Curriculum attainment targets' charts on pages 193–200.

Number – Number and place value

National Curriculum attainment target

- Count, read and write numbers to 100 in numerals; count in multiples of twos, fives and tens

Prerequisite checklist

Can the pupil:
- count reliably with numbers from 1 to 20?
- read and write numbers to 20 in numerals?
- recognise the numbers 1 to 100?

Success criteria

A. Read numbers to 100 in numerals
B. Write numbers to 100 in numerals
C. Count in multiples of 2
D. Count in multiples of 5
E. Count in multiples of 10

Resources

Resource 1: Numbers 1 to 20
Resource 2: Two-digit numbers
pencil and paper (per pupil)

NOTES

- To assess a pupil's mastery of counting on or back in ones, beginning with 0, 1 or any given number, to and across 100, refer to Assessment Task 1.
- Success criteria A and B of this Assessment Task assess the pupil's level of mastery in being able to read and write numbers to 100 in numerals. Success criteria A and B of Assessment Task 5 assess the pupil's mastery in being able to read and write numbers to 20 in numerals. Both sets of tasks are similar, therefore it is recommended that teachers assess a pupil's mastery in being able to read and write numbers to 20 in numerals first (Assessment Task 5), before extending this to numbers to 100 (Assessment Task 2).

Assessment Task

Success criterion A: Read numbers to 100 in numerals

What to do	What to say	What to look out for
Display Resources 1 and 2 and point to a number.	*What is this number?*	Can the pupil read numbers to 100 in numerals?
	Point to the number 42.	

Repeat until the pupil has sufficiently demonstrated their ability to read numbers to 100 in numerals.

Success criterion B: Write numbers to 100 in numerals

What to do	What to say	What to look out for
Provide the pupil with pencil and paper.	*Write down the number 27 as a [numeral/figure/number].*	Can the pupil write numbers to 100 in numerals?
	Tell me a different number less than 100. Write this number as a [numeral/figure].	

Repeat until the pupil has sufficiently demonstrated their ability to write numbers to 100 in numerals.

Success criterion C: Count in multiples of 2

What to do	What to say	What to look out for
	Starting from zero, count on in steps of two until I say stop. Ready? Go!	Can the pupil count to at least the 8th multiple of 2 (16)?

Success criterion D: Count in multiples of 5

What to do	What to say	What to look out for
	Starting from zero, count on in steps of five until I say stop. Ready? Go!	Can the pupil count to at least the 8th multiple of 5 (40)?

Success criterion E: Count in multiples of 10

What to do	What to say	What to look out for
	Starting from zero, count on in steps of ten until I say stop. Ready? Go!	Can the pupil count to at least the 8th multiple of 10 (80)?

What to do for those pupils working *below* or *above* expectations

Refer to the 'Tracking back and forward through the Mathematics National Curriculum attainment targets' charts on pages 193–200.

Number – Number and place value

National Curriculum attainment target

• Given a number, identify one more and one less

Prerequisite checklist

Can the pupil:
• count reliably with numbers from 1 to at least 20?
• say the number names in order from 1 to at least 20?
• recognise the numbers 1 to 100?

Success criteria

A. Find 1 more than a given number to 20
B. Find 1 less than a given number to 20
C. Find 1 more than a given two-digit number
D. Find 1 less than a given two-digit number

Resources

Resource 1: Numbers 1 to 20 (made into number cards)

Resource 2: Two-digit numbers (made into number cards)

NOTE

• Success criteria C and D involve two-digit numbers greater than 20 and are therefore extensions of Success criteria A and B. Only use Success criteria C and D for those pupils who successfully master Success criteria A and B.

Assessment Task

Success criterion A: Find 1 more than a given number to 20

What to do	What to say	What to look out for
Shuffle the number cards from Resource 1 and place them in a pile face down on the table. Turn over the top card.	*What number is this? What is one more than this number?*	Can the pupil say the number that is 1 more than a given number to 20?

Repeat until the pupil has sufficiently demonstrated their ability to say the number that is 1 more than a given number to 20.

Success criterion B: Find 1 less than a given number to 20

What to do	What to say	What to look out for
Shuffle the number cards from Resource 1 and place them in a pile face down on the table. Turn over the top card.	*What number is this? What is one less than [...]?*	Can the pupil say the number that is 1 less than a given number to 20?

Repeat until the pupil has sufficiently demonstrated their ability to say the number that is 1 less than a given number to 20.

Success criterion C: Find 1 more than a given two-digit number

What to do	What to say	What to look out for
Shuffle the number cards from Resource 2 and place them in a pile face down on the table. Turn over the top card.	*What number is this? What is one more than [...]?*	Can the pupil say the number that is 1 more than a given two-digit number?

Repeat until the pupil has sufficiently demonstrated their ability to say the number that is 1 more than a given two-digit number.

Success criterion D: Find 1 less than a given two-digit number

What to do	What to say	What to look out for
Shuffle the number cards from Resource 2 and place them in a pile face down on the table. Turn over the top card.	*What number is this? What is one less than this number?*	Can the pupil say the number that is 1 less than a given two-digit number?

Repeat until the pupil has sufficiently demonstrated their ability to say the number that is 1 less than a given two-digit number.

What to do for those pupils working *below* or *above* expectations

Refer to the 'Tracking back and forward through the Mathematics National Curriculum attainment targets' charts on pages 193–200.

Number – Number and place value

National Curriculum attainment target

- Identify and represent numbers using objects and pictorial representations including the number line, and use the language of: equal to, more than, less than (fewer), most, least

Prerequisite checklist

Can the pupil:

- count reliably with numbers from 1 to at least 20?
- say the number names in order from 1 to at least 20?
- recognise the numbers 1 to at least 20?

Success criteria

A. Count reliably at least 20 objects
B. Use the language of 'equal to', 'more', 'less', 'fewer', 'most' and 'least' to compare sets of objects
C. Identify numbers using objects and pictorial representations
D. Represent numbers using objects and pictorial representations

E. Understand and use the language of comparing numbers to at least 20
F. Understand and use the language of ordering a set of numbers to at least 20

Resources

4–5 different containers, each holding about 30 of the *same* counting object, e.g. counters, cubes, beads, buttons or Compare Bears

Resource 5: Identifying numbers

two sets of Resource 1: Numbers 1 to 20 (made into number cards)

two sets of Resource 2: Two-digit numbers (made into number cards) (optional)

selection of 1 p, 5 p and 10 p coins

Base 10 material (optional)

pencil and paper (per pupil)

NOTES

- Only use Base 10 material if the pupil is familiar with this resource.
- All the Success criteria for this Assessment Task involve working with numbers to 20. If a pupil has demonstrated that they have mastered working with numbers to 20, increase the number range to include numbers to 100.

Assessment Task

Success criterion A: Count reliably at least 20 objects

What to do	What to say	What to look out for
Place one of the containers holding the counting objects (e.g. the counters) in front of the pupil.		
Ask the pupil to take a handful of the objects and place them on the table.	*How many counters do you think there are?* *How could you find out?*	Can the pupil count reliably at least 20 objects?
Allow the pupil sufficient time to count the objects.		
Once the pupil has done this, reorganise the objects into a pile again.	*How many counters are there now?* *Is the number of counters still the same?* *How do you know?*	Does the pupil recognise that when rearranged the number of objects stays the same?
Collect the objects and place them back into the container.		

Continue until the pupil has sufficiently demonstrated their ability to count reliably at least 20 objects. Where appropriate, encourage the pupil to count the number of objects without touching them.

Success criterion B: Use the language of 'equal to', 'more', 'less', 'fewer', 'most' and 'least' to compare sets of objects

What to do	What to say	What to look out for
Take a handful of counting objects (e.g. counters and cubes) from two of the containers and place them in front of the pupil, ensuring there are different numbers of each.	*Look at these counters and cubes. Do you think there are more counters or more cubes? How will you find out for sure? So, are there more counters or cubes?*	Can the pupil identify which group of objects there are more of?
Collect the objects and place them back into their respective containers.		
Repeat above asking the pupil to identify which object there is less/fewer of.	*Look at these buttons and beads. Do you think there are [less/fewer] buttons or beads? So, are there [less/fewer] buttons or beads?*	Can the pupil identify which group of objects there are less/fewer of?
Collect the objects and place them back into their respective containers.		
Place two containers near the pupil, e.g. Compare Bears and beads, and take a handful of objects from one of the containers and place them in front of the pupil, e.g. Compare Bears.	*How many Compare Bears are there? I want you to give me more beads than this.*	Can the pupil provide a set of objects that is more than another set of objects?
Place a third container in front of the pupil, e.g. buttons.	*How many Compare Bears did you say you have? Now I want you to give me [less/fewer] buttons than Compare Bears.*	Can the pupil provide a set of objects that is less/fewer than another set of objects?
Place a fourth container in front of the pupil, e.g. counters.	*How many Compare Bears do you have? Will you give me the same number of counters as you have Compare Bears?*	Can the pupil provide a set of objects that is the same number as another set of objects?
Ensure that the four different piles of counting objects are in front of the pupil.	*Look at the piles of Compare Bears, beads, buttons and counters. Which object do you have the most of? Which object do you have the least of? What can you say about the number of Compare Bears and counters that you have?*	Does the pupil understand the terms 'most', 'least' and 'the same' when comparing sets of objects?

Success criterion C: Identify numbers using objects and pictorial representations

What to do	What to say	What to look out for
Display Resource 5 and point to one of the groups of objects, e.g. 1 p coins, cubes, books and pegs.	*How many 1 p coins are there? Can you point to this number on the number line?*	Can the pupil correctly count the number of objects? Does the pupil correctly identify the number on the number line?
Point to one of the numbers on the number line that represents the number of one of the groups of objects on the sheet, e.g. 14 for the number of beads on the string.	*What is this number? One of the groups on this sheet has 14 objects in it. Which group of objects is it?*	Can the pupil correctly identify the number of objects?

Repeat above for other groups of objects until the pupil has sufficiently demonstrated their ability to identify numbers using objects and pictorial representations.

Success criterion D: Represent numbers using objects and pictorial representations

What to do	What to say	What to look out for
Place the following near the pupil: – one of the containers holding the counting objects, e.g. the buttons – selection of 1 p, 5 p and 10 p coins – Base 10 material (optional) – pencil and paper – Display Resource 1 and point to a number, e.g. 14.	*What number is this? Can you give me 14 buttons?* *Can you give me 14p using these coins?* *[optional] How would you make 14 using the Base 10 material?* *Could you draw me 14 apples?*	Can the pupil represent numbers using objects and pictorial representations?

Repeat above until the pupil has sufficiently demonstrated their ability to represent numbers using objects and pictorial representations.

Success criterion E: Understand and use the language of comparing numbers to at least 20

What to do	What to say	What to look out for
Shuffle one set of number cards from Resource 1 and lay two non-consecutive cards face up in front of the pupil. Ask questions similar to the ones shown here:	*Look at the cards in front of you. Which number is [more/less]?* *Point to the [bigger/larger/smaller] number.* *Tell me a number between your two numbers.* *Can you tell me another number that lies between these two numbers?*	Can the pupil compare two numbers to at least 20 using language such as 'more than' and 'less than'? Can the pupil say a number that lies between two other numbers?
Using a card from the second set of number cards from Resource 1, lay two identical number cards face up in front of the pupil, e.g. 12 and 12.	*Look at these two numbers. Which number is [more/less]?*	Can the pupil compare two numbers to at least 20 using language such as 'equal to' and 'the same as'?

Repeat above using other pairs of numbers, asking questions similar to those above, until the pupil has sufficiently demonstrated that they understand and can use the language of comparing numbers to 20.
If appropriate, repeat above using the two-digit number cards from Resource 2.

Success criterion F: Understand and use the language of ordering a set of numbers to at least 20

What to do	What to say	What to look out for
Lay four consecutive number cards from Resource 1 face up in front of the pupil, making sure that the numbers are not in order, e.g. 7, 9, 6 and 8.	*Look at the numbers in front of you. I want you to place these cards in order, smallest to largest.*	Can the pupil order a set of four consecutive numbers from 1 to 20?
Lay four non-consecutive number cards from Resource 1 face up in front of the pupil, making sure that the numbers are not in order, e.g. 14, 3, 19 and 10.	*Look at the numbers in front of you. I want you to place these numbers in order, smallest to largest.*	Can the pupil order a set of four and then five non-consecutive numbers from 1 to 20?
Once the pupil has done this give them another card.	*Look at the cards you have just put in order. Where would you put this number so that the order is still correct?*	

Repeat above using other sets of numbers, asking questions similar to those above, until the pupil has sufficiently demonstrated they understand and can use the language of ordering numbers to 20.
If appropriate, repeat above for ordering non-consecutive numbers using the two-digit number cards from Resource 2.

What to do for those pupils working *below* or *above* expectations

Refer to the 'Tracking back and forward through the Mathematics National Curriculum attainment targets' charts on pages 193–200.

Number – Number and place value

National Curriculum attainment target

- Read and write numbers from 1 to 20 in numerals and words

Prerequisite checklist

Can the pupil:
- count reliably with numbers from 1 to 20?
- recognise numbers of personal significance?

Success criteria

A. Read numbers to 20 in numerals
B. Write numbers to 20 in numerals
C. Read numbers to 20 in words
D. Write numbers to 20 in words

Resources

Resource 1: Numbers 1 to 20
Resource 4: Numbers 0 to 20 in words
pencil and paper (per pupil)

NOTE

- Success criteria A and B of this Assessment Task assess the pupil's level of mastery in being able to read and write numbers to 20 in numerals. Success criteria A and B of Assessment Task 2 assess the pupil's mastery in being able to read and write numbers to 100 in numerals. Both sets of tasks are similar, therefore it is recommended that teachers assess a pupil's mastery in being able to read and write numbers to 20 in numerals first (Assessment Task 5), before extending this to numbers to 100 (Assessment Task 2).

Assessment Task

Success criterion A: Read numbers to 20 in numerals

What to do	What to say	What to look out for
Display Resource 1 and point to a number.	*What is this number?*	Can the pupil read numbers to 20 in numerals?
	Point to the number 13.	

Repeat until the pupil has sufficiently demonstrated their ability to read numbers to 20 in numerals.

Success criterion B: Write numbers to 20 in numerals

What to do	What to say	What to look out for
Provide the pupil with pencil and paper.	*Write down the number eight as a [number/numeral/figure].*	Can the pupil write numbers to 20 in numerals?
	Tell me a different number less than 20. Write this number as a [numeral/figure].	

Repeat until the pupil has sufficiently demonstrated their ability to write numbers to 20 in numerals.

Success criterion C: Read numbers to 20 in words

What to do	What to say	What to look out for
Display Resource 4 and point to a number.	*What is this number?*	Can the pupil read numbers to 20 in words?
	Point to the number 18.	

Repeat until the pupil has sufficiently demonstrated their ability to read numbers to 20 in words.

Success criterion D: Write numbers to 20 in words

What to do	What to say	What to look out for
Provide the pupil with pencil and paper.	*Write down the number 16 as a word.*	Can the pupil write numbers to 20 in words?
	Tell me a different number less than 20. *Write this number as a word.*	

Repeat until the pupil has sufficiently demonstrated their ability to write numbers to 20 in words.

What to do for those pupils working *below* or *above* expectations

Refer to the 'Tracking back and forward through the Mathematics National Curriculum attainment targets' charts on pages 193–200.

Number – Addition and subtraction

National Curriculum attainment target

- Read, write and interpret mathematical statements involving addition (+), subtraction (–) and equals (=) signs

Prerequisite checklist

Can the pupil:

- demonstrate an understanding of the concept of addition?
- demonstrate an understanding of the concept of subtraction?
- use quantities and objects to add two one-digit numbers and count on to find the answer?
- use quantities and objects to subtract two one-digit numbers and count on or back to find the answer?

Success criteria

A. Read and interpret addition calculations
B. Write addition calculations
C. Read and interpret subtraction calculations
D. Write subtraction calculations

Resources

4–5 different containers, each holding about 30 of the *same* counting object, e.g. counters, cubes, beads, buttons or Compare Bears

Resource 6: Addition number facts to 10 (enlarged to A3 and made into cards)

Resource 7: Subtraction number facts to 10 (enlarged to A3 and made into cards)

Resource 8: Addition number facts 11 to 20 (enlarged to A3 and made into cards)

Resource 9: Subtraction number facts 11 to 20 (enlarged to A3 and made into cards)

sheet of paper with two large rings drawn on one side, i.e.

and one large ring drawn on the other side of the sheet, i.e.

pencil and two sheets of paper (per pupil)

NOTE

- In keeping with the other Year 1 National Curriculum attainment targets for Number – Addition and subtraction, all of the calculations in this Assessment Task involve representing and using addition facts and related subtraction facts to 20. Tasks begin with number facts to 10 (Resources 6 and 7) and then increase to number facts from 11 to 20 (Resources 8 and 9). If necessary, maintain the number facts involved to 10.

Assessment Task

Success criterion A: Read and interpret addition calculations

What to do	What to say	What to look out for
Place one of the containers holding the counting objects in front of the pupil, e.g. the Compare Bears. Place one of the addition number facts to 10 cards from Resource 6 in front of the pupil, e.g. $3 + 5 = \square$.	*Can you read this number fact to me?* *What does it mean?* *Can you use these Compare Bears to tell me a story about this number fact?*	Can the pupil read and interpret the addition calculation?

Repeat several times until the pupil has sufficiently demonstrated their ability to read and interpret addition calculations. If appropriate, use the addition number facts 11 to 20 on Resource 8.

Success criterion B: Write addition calculations

What to do	What to say	What to look out for
Place the sheet of paper with the two rings in front of the pupil and given them another sheet of paper and a pencil. Take 4 of the counting objects from one of the containers, e.g. 4 counters, and place them in one of the rings drawn on the sheet of paper. Then take another 2 of the same object and place these in the second ring, i.e. 	*How many counters are there here?* *And how many counters are there here?* *How many counters are there altogether?* *On your sheet of paper can you write a number sentence for this?*	Can the pupil write an addition calculation for a given situation?

Repeat several times until the pupil has sufficiently demonstrated their ability to write addition calculations. If appropriate, create situations that involve addition number facts from 11 to 20.

Success criterion C: Read and interpret subtraction calculations

What to do	What to say	What to look out for
Place another of the containers holding the counting objects in front of the pupil, e.g. the buttons. Place one of the subtraction number facts to 10 cards from Resource 7 in front of the pupil, e.g. 9 – 3 = □.	*Can you read this number fact to me?* *What does it mean?* *Can you use these buttons to tell me a story about this number fact?*	Can the pupil read and interpret the subtraction calculation?

Repeat several times until the pupil has sufficiently demonstrated their ability to read and interpret subtraction calculations. If appropriate, use the subtraction number facts 11 to 20 on Resource 9.

Success criterion D: Write subtraction calculations

What to do	What to say	What to look out for
Place the sheet of paper with one ring in front of the pupil and give them another sheet of paper and a pencil. Take 6 of the counting objects from one of the containers, e.g. 6 beads, and place them in the ring drawn on the sheet of paper, i.e. 	*How many beads are there?*	
Remove 2 of the beads from inside the ring and place them beside the sheet of paper, i.e. 	*How many beads have I taken from the sheet of paper?* *How many beads are left on the sheet of paper?* *On your sheet of paper can you write a number sentence for this?*	Can the pupil write a subtraction calculation for a given situation?

Repeat several times until the pupil has sufficiently demonstrated their ability to write subtraction calculations. If appropriate, create situations that involve subtraction number facts from 11 to 20.

What to do for those pupils working *below* or *above* expectations

Refer to the 'Tracking back and forward through the Mathematics National Curriculum attainment targets' charts on pages 193–200.

Number – Addition and subtraction

National Curriculum attainment target

- Represent and use number bonds and related subtraction facts within 20

Prerequisite checklist

Can the pupil:

- demonstrate an understanding of the concept of addition?
- demonstrate an understanding of the concept of subtraction?
- use quantities and objects to add two one-digit numbers and count on to find the answer?
- use quantities and objects to subtract two one-digit numbers and count on or back to find the answer?
- read, write and interpret mathematical statements involving addition (+), subtraction (–) and equals (=) signs?

Success criteria

A. Recall addition number facts to 10
B. Recall addition number facts from 11 to 20
C. Recall subtraction number facts to 10
D. Recall subtraction number facts from 11 to 20
E. Recall addition and subtraction number facts to 20, and understand the associated vocabulary

Resources

Resource 1: Numbers 1 to 20 (enlarged to A3 and made into cards)

Resource 6: Addition number facts to 10 (enlarged to A3 and made into cards)

Resource 7: Subtraction number facts to 10 (enlarged to A3 and made into cards)

Resource 8: Addition number facts 11 to 20 (enlarged to A3 and made into cards)

Resource 9: Subtraction number facts 11 to 20 (enlarged to A3 and made into cards)

2 small different coloured counters

Assessment Task

Success criterion A: Recall addition number facts to 10

What to do	What to say	What to look out for
Place the addition number facts to 10 cards from Resource 6 in a pile face down on the table.	I'm going to show you some addition number facts and I want you to answer them as quickly as you can. Ready? Let's begin!	
Turn over the top card.		Can the pupil recall addition number facts to 10?
Repeat several times.		

Success criterion B: Recall addition number facts from 11 to 20

What to do	What to say	What to look out for
Place the addition number facts from 11 to 20 cards from Resource 8 in a pile face down on the table.	I'm going to show you some more addition number facts and I want you to answer them as quickly as you can. Ready? Let's go!	
Turn over the top card.		Can the pupil recall addition number facts from 11 to 20?
Repeat several times.		

Success criterion C: Recall subtraction number facts to 10

What to do	What to say	What to look out for
Place the subtraction number facts to 10 cards from Resource 7 in a pile face down on the table.	*I'm going to show you some subtraction number facts and I want you to answer them as quickly as you can. Ready? Let's begin!*	
Turn over the top card.		Can the pupil recall subtraction number facts to 10?
Repeat several times.		

Success criterion D: Recall subtraction number facts from 11 to 20

What to do	What to say	What to look out for
Place the subtraction number facts from 11 to 20 cards from Resource 9 in a pile face down on the table.	*I'm going to show you some more subtraction number facts and again I want you to answer them as quickly as you can. Ready? Let's go!*	
Turn over the top card.		Can the pupil recall subtraction number facts from 11 to 20?
Repeat several times.		

Success criterion E: Recall addition and subtraction number facts to 20, and understand the associated vocabulary

What to do	What to say	What to look out for
Shuffle the 1 to 20 number cards from Resource 1, and spread them out face up on the table.	*Look at these number cards. I'm going to place these two counters onto two cards. I'm then going to say an instruction. It might be: 'Add these two numbers together' or 'What is the total of these two numbers?' or 'Find the difference between these two numbers'. You have to tell me the answer as quickly as you can. Ready?*	
Place the counters onto two number cards where the total is 20 or less, e.g. 13 and 4. Say a phrase similar to the ones shown here, ensuring that you use a range of different vocabulary, e.g. add, plus, sum, total, more, difference between, subtract, take away, minus, less and fewer.	*– What is the total of these two numbers?* *– What is the sum of these two numbers?* *– What is 13 plus 4?* *– Add these two numbers together.* *– What is 13 minus 4?* *– What is 4 less than 13?* *– Take away the smaller number from the larger number.* *– What is the difference between these two numbers?*	Can the pupil recall addition and subtraction number facts to 20?

Continue until the pupil has sufficiently demonstrated their ability to recall addition and subtraction number facts to 20, as well as their understanding of the vocabulary associated with addition and subtraction.

What to do for those pupils working *below* or *above* expectations

Refer to the 'Tracking back and forward through the Mathematics National Curriculum attainment targets' charts on pages 193–200.

Number – Addition and subtraction

National Curriculum attainment target

- Add and subtract one-digit and two-digit numbers to 20, including zero

Prerequisite checklist

Can the pupil:

- demonstrate an understanding of the concept of addition?
- demonstrate an understanding of the concept of subtraction?
- use quantities and objects to add two one-digit numbers and count on to find the answer?
- use quantities and objects to subtract two one-digit numbers and count on or back to find the answer?
- read, write and interpret mathematical statements involving addition (+), subtraction (–) and equals (=) signs?

Success criteria

A. Add a one-digit number (including zero) to a two-digit number to 20

B. Subtract a one-digit number (including zero) from a two-digit number to 20

C. Add and subtract a one-digit number (including zero) to and from a two-digit number to 20, and understand the associated vocabulary

Resources

Resource 10: Numbers 11 to 20

0–9 dice

small counter

Assessment Task

Success criterion A: Add a one-digit number (including zero) to a two-digit number to 20

What to do	What to say	What to look out for
Place Resource 10 and the dice on the table in front of the pupil.	*I want you to roll this dice. I'm then going to put a counter on one of the cats. Then I want you to add the dice number to the number that the cat is holding. Ready?*	
After the pupil has rolled the dice, place the counter on one of the cats.	*Add these two numbers together.*	Can the pupil add a one-digit number (including 0) to a two-digit number to 20?

Continue until the pupil has sufficiently demonstrated their ability to add a one-digit number (including 0) to a two-digit number to 20.

Success criterion B: Subtract a one-digit number (including zero) from a two-digit number to 20

What to do	What to say	What to look out for
	Now I want you to subtract the dice number from the number that the cat is holding. Ready?	
After the pupil has rolled the dice, place the counter on one of the cats.	*What is […] [take away/subtract] […]?*	Can the pupil subtract a one-digit number (including 0) from a two-digit number to 20?

Continue until the pupil has sufficiently demonstrated their ability to subtract a one-digit number (including 0) from a two-digit number to 20.

Success criterion C: Add and subtract a one-digit number (including zero) to and from a two-digit number to 20, and understand the associated vocabulary

What to do	What to say	What to look out for
	This time after you roll the dice and I have put a counter on one of the cats, I'm going to tell you whether to add the dice number to the number that the cat is holding, or subtract the dice number from the number the cat is holding. I want you to try to give me the answer as quickly as you can. Ready? Let's go!	
After the pupil has rolled the dice, place the counter on one of the cats. Say a phrase/ask a question similar to the ones shown here, ensuring that you use a range of different vocabulary, e.g. add, plus, sum, total, more, difference between, subtract, take away, minus, less and fewer.	– *What is the total of these two numbers?* – *What is the sum of these two numbers?* – *What is 15 plus 3?* – *Add these two numbers together.* – *What is 15 minus 3?* – *What is 3 less than 15?* – *Take away the smaller number from the larger number.* – *What is the difference between these two numbers?*	Can the pupil add and subtract a one-digit number (including 0) to and from a two-digit number to 20?

Continue until the pupil has sufficiently demonstrated their ability to add and subtract a one-digit number (including 0) to and from a two-digit number to 20, as well as their understanding of the vocabulary associated with addition and subtraction.

What to do for those pupils working *below* or *above* expectations

Refer to the 'Tracking back and forward through the Mathematics National Curriculum attainment targets' charts on pages 193–200.

Number – Addition and subtraction

National Curriculum attainment target

- Solve one-step problems that involve addition and subtraction, using concrete objects and pictorial representations, and missing number problems such as $7 = \square - 9$

Prerequisite checklist

Can the pupil:

- demonstrate an understanding of the concept of addition?
- demonstrate an understanding of the concept of subtraction?
- read, write and interpret mathematical statements involving addition (+), subtraction (–) and equals (=) signs?
- recall addition and subtraction number facts to 20?

Success criteria

A. Solve one-step problems that involve addition and subtraction, using concrete objects and pictorial representations
B. Solve missing number problems

Resources

Resource 1: Numbers 1 to 20 (made into number cards)
Resource 11: Problem-solving plates (enlarged to A3)
Resource 12: Problem-solving pictures
Resource 13: Signs and shapes cards

NOTES

- You may wish to substitute the plates on Resource 11 for real or paper plates if these are readily available.
- Prior to the Assessment Task:
  - Cut out the 1 to 20 number cards from Resource 1. Shuffle the cards and place them in a pile.
  - Cut out both plates from Resource 11.
  - Cut out all the pictures of food from Resource 12. Place each of the different types of food into separate piles.
  - Cut out all the signs and shapes from Resource 13. Place each of the different signs into separate piles, and all the shapes into one pile.

Assessment Task

Success criterion A: Solve one-step problems that involve addition and subtraction, using concrete objects and pictorial representations

What to do	What to say	What to look out for
Place the two plates on the table in front of the pupil.		
Place 3 apples on one plate and 2 apples on the other plate. Ask questions similar to the ones shown here:	– How many apples are there on this plate? How many apples are there on this plate? – Which plate has [more/less]? How many [more/less]? – How many apples are there altogether on these two plates?	Can the pupil solve simple problems that involve counting objects of the same type?
Repeat above using other pictures of the same type.		
Place 2 slices of pizza on one plate and 4 cupcakes on the other plate. Ask questions similar to the ones shown here:	– How many slices of pizza are there on this plate? – How many cakes are there on this plate? – Are there [more/less] pizza slices or cupcakes on the plates? How many [more/less]? – How many slices of pizza and cakes are there altogether on these two plates?	Can the pupil solve simple problems that involve counting different types of objects?
Repeat above using other combinations of different pictures.		

What to do	What to say	What to look out for
Place 5 sandwiches on one of the plates. Ask questions similar to the ones shown here:	– *How many sandwiches are there on this plate?* – *If I put another [one/two/three/four] sandwiches on this plate, how many would that be altogether?* – *If I ate [one/two/three/four/all of these] sandwiches how many would be left?*	Can the pupil solve one-step addition and subtraction problems?
After you have asked a question, occasionally follow this up with another question that will elicit from the pupil their mental method. Ask questions similar to the ones shown here:	– *How did you get that answer?* – *What picture did you have in your head?* – *How else could you have worked it out? Is there another way?*	Can the pupil use and explain mental strategies to solve one-step addition and subtraction problems?

Repeat above, using other pictures and combinations of different pictures until the pupil has sufficiently demonstrated their ability to solve one-step problems that involve addition and subtraction, using concrete objects and pictorial representations.

Success criterion B: Solve missing number problems

What to do	What to say	What to look out for
Place the separate piles of 1 to 20 number cards from Resource 1 and the signs and shapes cards from Resource 13 on the table.		
Use the cards to create an addition or subtraction missing number problem, e.g. $4 + \square = 9$ $\quad 10 = \square + 6$ $\bigcirc + 3 = 7$ $\quad 8 = 7 + \diamond$ $8 - \diamond = 6$ $\quad 3 = \bigcirc - 5$ $\triangle - 5 = 1$ $\quad 4 = 6 - \triangle$ Ask questions similar to the ones shown here:	– *Can you tell me the value of the square?* – *What should replace the circle to complete this number sentence?* – *Which card do you need to replace the circle card with to make this number sentence true?*	Can the pupil work out the missing number to complete the calculation?
Instruct the pupil to use the remaining 1 to 20 number cards to replace the shape card with the correct number card to complete the calculation.	*Use these other number cards to replace the shape card with the missing number.*	
After the pupil has answered a question, occasionally follow this up with a question that will elicit from the pupil their mental method. Ask questions similar to the ones shown here:	– *How did you get that answer?* – *What picture did you have in your head?* – *How else could you have worked it out? Is there another way?*	Can the pupil use and explain mental strategies to solve missing number problems?

Repeat above, creating a variety of addition and subtraction calculations with the unknown value in different positions in the number sentence until the pupil has sufficiently demonstrated their ability to solve missing number problems.

What to do for those pupils working *below* or *above* expectations
Refer to the 'Tracking back and forward through the Mathematics National Curriculum attainment targets' charts on pages 193–200.

Number – Multiplication and division

National Curriculum attainment target

- Solve one-step problems involving multiplication and division, by calculating the answer using concrete objects, pictorial representations and arrays with the support of the teacher

Prerequisite checklist

Can the pupil:

- solve problems that involve combining groups of 2, 5 or 10?
- solve problems that involve sharing into equal groups?
- solve problems involving doubling and halving?

Success criteria

A. Understand multiplication using arrays
B. Solve problems that involve combining groups of 2, 5 or 10 using concrete objects and pictorial representations
C. Understand division as 'sharing'
D. Understand division as 'grouping'
E. Solve problems that involve sharing objects into equal groups using concrete objects and pictorial representations

Resources

Resource 14: Array cards

two copies of Resource 15: Combining groups of 2, 5 or 10

two copies of Resource 16: Sharing into equal groups: sheep (alternatively, if available use plastic farm animals)

two copies of Resource 17: Sharing into equal groups: fields (enlarged to A3)

several sheets of A4 paper

counters

NOTE

- Prior to the Assessment Task:
  - Cut out the array cards from Resource 14. Place them in a pile.
  - Cut out the picture cards from Resource 15. Place each of the different types of fruit into separate piles.
  - Place the 70 sheep from Resource 16 into a pile.

Assessment Task

Success criterion A: Understand multiplication using arrays

What to do	What to say	What to look out for
Place one of the array cards from Resource 14 in front of the pupil, e.g. Ask questions similar to the ones shown here:	– How many dots are there in each row? – How many rows are there? – How many dots are there altogether? – How can you work it out without counting all the dots?	Can the pupil use an array to describe multiplication?

Repeat above using other array cards until the pupil has sufficiently demonstrated their understanding of multiplication using arrays.

Success criterion B: Solve problems that involve combining groups of 2, 5 or 10 using concrete objects and pictorial representations

What to do	What to say	What to look out for
Place several picture cards of the same type from Resource 15 in front of the pupil, i. e.	*There are five bananas in each 'hand'. How many bananas are there altogether?*	Can the pupil combine groups of 2, 5 or 10 and find out how many there are altogether?
Repeat above using the other picture cards from Resource 15, asking questions similar to the ones shown here:	*– There are ten grapes in each bunch. How many grapes are there altogether in these four bunches?* *– How many cherries are there altogether in eight bunches? Use the cherries to show me.*	
Occasionally ask the pupil to explain how they worked out the answer.	*– How did you work that out?* *– How did you get that answer?* *– How did you know that there are that many grapes?* *– How can you work it out without counting them all?*	

Continue until the pupil has sufficiently demonstrated that they can solve problems that involve combining groups of 2, 5 or 10.

Success criterion C: Understand division as 'sharing'

What to do	What to say	What to look out for
Draw three rings on one of the sheets of A4 paper and place 12 counters near the paper, i.e.	*How many counters are there? I want you to share these 12 counters equally between three groups.*	Can the pupil share out equally a quantity into a given number of groups?
	So, how many counters are there in each group?	

Repeat above drawing a different number of rings and using a different number of counters until the pupil has sufficiently demonstrated their understanding of division as 'sharing'.

Success criterion D: Understand division as 'grouping'

What to do	What to say	What to look out for
Place 15 counters on the table in front of the pupil.	*How many counters are there? I want you to arrange these counters into groups of five.*	Can the pupil work out how many equal groups there are for a given quantity?
	So, how many groups of five counters are there in 15?	

Repeat above using a different number of counters and asking the pupil to arrange them into groups of a different size until the pupil has sufficiently demonstrated their understanding of division as 'grouping'.

Success criterion E: Solve problems that involve sharing objects into equal groups using concrete objects and pictorial representations

What to do	What to say	What to look out for
Fold one of the sheets of 5 fields from Resource 17, so that only two fields are visible. Place 8 sheep beside the 2 fields, e.g.	*How many sheep are there?* *How many fields are there?* *I want you to share these eight sheep equally between these two fields.*	Can the pupil share out equally a quantity into a given number of groups?
	So, how many sheep are there in each field?	

Repeat above asking the pupil to share one or more of the following:
  – a multiple of 2 sheep between 2 fields;
  – a multiple of 3 sheep between 3 fields;
  – a multiple of 4 sheep between 4 fields;
  – a multiple of 5 sheep between 5 fields;
  – a multiple of 10 sheep between 10 fields.
Continue until the pupil has sufficiently demonstrated that they can solve practical problems that involve sharing objects into equal groups.

What to do for those pupils working *below* or *above* expectations

Refer to the 'Tracking back and forward through the Mathematics National Curriculum attainment targets' charts on pages 193–200.

Number – Fractions

National Curriculum attainment target

- Recognise, find and name one half as one of two equal parts of an object, shape or quantity

Prerequisite checklist

Can the pupil:
- solve problems involving doubling and halving?
- use the vocabulary of halves in context?

Success criteria

A. Understand the concept of 'half'
B. Find half of a shape
C. Find half of a group of objects
D. Find half of a number

Resources

some paper shapes, e.g. squares, rectangles, triangles and circles

Resource 18: Halves and quarters (1) (per pupil)

Resource 19: Halves and quarters (2)

coloured pencil (per pupil)

collection of counting objects, e.g. counters, cubes and buttons

Assessment Task

Success criterion A: Understand the concept of 'half'

What to do	What to say	What to look out for
Provide the pupil with a paper shape and ask them to fold the shape in half.	*Look at this square. I want you to fold it in half.*	Can the pupil fold the shape in half?
Once the pupil has done this, ask them to colour half of the shape.	*Now I want you to colour half of the shape.*	Can the pupil colour half of the shape?

Repeat above asking the pupil to fold and colour half of another shape. Continue until the pupil has sufficiently demonstrated their understanding of the concept of 'half'.

Success criterion B: Find half of a shape

What to do	What to say	What to look out for
Referring to Shape A on Resource 18, ask the pupil to colour half of the shape.	*Look at this circle, I want you to colour half of it for me.*	Can the pupil colour half of the shape?
Repeat above for Shape B.	*Look at this shape. Colour half of it for me.*	
Referring to Shape C, ask the pupil to divide the shape in half and then to colour half of the shape.	*Look at this triangle. Draw a line through the triangle so that it is divided in half. Now colour half of the triangle.*	Can the pupil divide the shape in half?
Repeat above for Shape D.	*Look at the square. Draw a line through the square so that it is divided in half and then colour half of the square.*	Can the pupil colour half of the shape?

Success criterion C: Find half of a group of objects

What to do	What to say	What to look out for
Referring to the groups of objects at the bottom of Resource 18, ask the pupil to circle half of the trucks.	*Look at this group of trucks. I want you to circle half of them.*	Can the pupil find half of a group of objects?
Repeat above asking the pupil to circle half of the aeroplanes.	*Look at this group of planes. Circle half of them.*	

If necessary, use the collection of counting objects to show other groups of objects in multiples of 2, and ask the pupil to find half of the objects. Repeat until the pupil has sufficiently demonstrated their ability to find half of a group of objects.

Success criterion D: Find half of a number

What to do	What to say	What to look out for
Place Resource 19 on the table in front of the pupil.		
Point to one of the numbers and ask the pupil to find half of that number.	*What is half of 12?*	Can the pupil find half of a number?

Repeat above pointing to other numbers on the boats until the pupil has sufficiently demonstrated their ability to find half of a number.

What to do for those pupils working *below* or *above* expectations

Refer to the 'Tracking back and forward through the Mathematics National Curriculum attainment targets' charts on pages 193–200.

Number – Fractions

National Curriculum attainment target

- Recognise, find and name one quarter as one of four equal parts of an object, shape or quantity

Prerequisite checklist

Can the pupil:

- solve problems involving doubling and halving?
- use the vocabulary of halves and quarters in context?

Success criteria

A. Understand the concept of 'quarter'

B. Find one quarter of a shape

C. Find one quarter of a group of objects

D. Find one quarter of a number

Resources

some paper shapes, e.g. squares, rectangles, triangles and circles

Resource 18: Halves and quarters (1) (per pupil)

Resource 19: Halves and quarters (2)

coloured pencil (per pupil)

collection of counting objects, e.g. counters, cubes and buttons

Assessment Task

Success criterion A: Understand the concept of 'quarter'

What to do	What to say	What to look out for
Provide the pupil with a paper shape and ask them to fold the shape into quarters.	*Look at this square. I want you to fold it into quarters.*	Can the pupil fold the shape into quarters?
Once the pupil has done this, ask them to colour one quarter of the shape.	*Now I want you to colour one quarter of the shape.*	Can the pupil colour one quarter of the shape?

Repeat above asking the pupil to fold and colour one quarter of another shape. Continue until the pupil has sufficiently demonstrated their understanding of the concept of 'quarter'.

Success criterion B: Find one quarter of a shape

What to do	What to say	What to look out for
Referring to Shape E on Resource 18, ask the pupil to colour one quarter of the shape.	*Look at this rectangle. I want you to colour quarter of it for me.*	Can the pupil colour one quarter of the shape?
Repeat above for Shape F.	*Look at this triangle. Colour one quarter of it for me.*	
Referring to Shape G, ask the pupil to divide the shape into quarters and then to colour one quarter of the shape.	*Look at this circle. I want you divide this circle into quarters.* *Now colour one quarter of the circle.*	Can the pupil divide the shape into quarters? Can the pupil colour one quarter of the shape?
Repeat above for Shape H	*Look at the square. Divide the square in quarters, then colour one quarter of the square.*	

Success criterion C: Find one quarter of a group of objects

What to do	What to say	What to look out for
Referring to the groups of objects at the bottom of Resource 18, ask the pupil to circle one quarter of the trains.	*Look at this group of trains. I want you to circle one quarter of them.*	Can the pupil find one quarter of a group of objects?
Repeat above asking the pupil to circle one quarter of the cars.	*Look at this group of cars. Circle one quarter of them.*	

If necessary, use the collection of counting objects to show other groups of objects in multiples of four, and ask the pupil to find one quarter of the objects. Repeat until the pupil has sufficiently demonstrated their ability to find one quarter of a group of objects.

Success criterion D: Find one quarter of a number

What to do	What to say	What to look out for
Place Resource 19 on the table in front of the pupil.		
Point to one of the numbers that is a multiple of four, e.g. 4, 8, 12, 16, 20, 24, 28 or 40, and ask the pupil to find one quarter of that number.	*What is one quarter of 12?*	Can the pupil find one quarter of a number?

Repeat above pointing to other numbers on the boats that are multiples of four until the pupil has sufficiently demonstrated their ability to find one quarter of a number.

What to do for those pupils working *below* or *above* expectations

Refer to the 'Tracking back and forward through the Mathematics National Curriculum attainment targets' charts on pages 193–200.

Measurement

National Curriculum attainment target

- Compare, describe and solve practical problems for:
  - lengths and heights [for example, long/short, longer/shorter, tall/short, double/half]
  - mass/weight [for example, heavy/light, heavier than/light than]
  - capacity and volume [for example, full/empty, more than, less than, half, half-full, quarter]
  - time [for example, quicker, slower, earlier, later]

Prerequisite checklist

Can the pupil:

- order two or three items by length or height?
- order two or three items by weight?
- order two or three items by capacity?
- use everyday language related to time?

Success criteria

A. Compare lengths by direct comparison using appropriate language

B. Compare heights by direct comparison using appropriate language

C. Compare masses/weights by direct comparison using appropriate language

D. Compare capacities by direct comparison using appropriate language

E. Compare volumes by direct comparison using appropriate language

F. Compare time using appropriate language

Resources

Length and height:
- about 6 objects measuring from 10 cm to 1 m (ensure that the objects can be used to describe length and/or height)

Mass/weight:
- about 6 objects weighing from 1 kg to 5 kg

Capacity:
- about 6 empty containers of different shapes and sizes from 250 ml to 5 litres

Volume:
- 4 identical containers: one full of water, one half-full of water, one about one quarter-full of water and one empty

NOTE

- Given the difference between the four measures assessed in this Assessment Task, i.e. length and height, mass/weight, capacity and volume, and time, it is recommended that each measure is assessed seperately, at a different time.

Assessment Task

Success criterion A: Compare lengths by direct comparison using appropriate language

What to do	What to say	What to look out for
Place the objects of different lengths and heights in front of the pupil.		
Pointing to two objects that clearly show length, ask the pupil questions similar to the ones shown here:	– Which of these two objects is the [longer/shorter]? – Tell me about the length of these two objects. – Compare the length of these two objects.	Can the pupil compare the lengths of two objects?
Repeat for other pairs of objects.		
Pointing to one of the objects that clearly shows length, ask the pupil questions similar to the ones shown here:	– Point to an object that is [longer/shorter] than the [...]. – Tell me something else that is [longer/shorter] than [...]. – Which objects are [longer/shorter] than the [...]?	Can the pupil compare the length of one object to the lengths of several other objects?
Repeat for other objects.		

Success criterion B: Compare heights by direct comparison using appropriate language

What to do	What to say	What to look out for
Pointing to two objects that clearly show height, ask the pupil questions similar to the ones shown here: Repeat for other pairs of objects.	– Which of these two objects is the [taller/shorter]? – Tell me about the height of these two objects. – Compare the height of these two objects.	Can the pupil compare the heights of two objects?
Pointing to one of the objects that clearly shows height, ask the pupil questions similar to the ones shown here: Repeat for other objects.	– Point to something that is [taller/shorter] than the [...]. – Tell me something else that is [taller/shorter] than [...]. – Which objects are [taller/shorter] than the [...]?	Can the pupil compare the height of one object to the heights of several other objects?

Success criterion C: Compare masses/weights by direct comparison using appropriate language

What to do	What to say	What to look out for
Place the objects of different masses/weights in front of the pupil.		
Pointing to two objects, ask the pupil questions similar to the ones shown here: Repeat for other pairs of objects.	– Which of these two objects is the [heavier/lighter]? – Tell me about the weight of these two objects. – Compare the weight of these two objects.	Can the pupil compare the masses of two objects?
Pointing to one of the objects, ask the pupil questions similar to the ones shown here: Repeat for other objects.	– Point to an object that is [heavier/lighter] than the [...]. – Tell me something else that is [heavier/lighter] than the [...]. – Which objects are [heavier/lighter] than the [...]?	Can the pupil compare the mass of one object to the masses of several other objects?

Success criterion D: Compare capacities by direct comparison using appropriate language

What to do	What to say	What to look out for
Place the empty containers of different shapes and sizes in front of the pupil.		
Pointing to two containers, ask the pupil questions similar to the ones shown here: Repeat for other pairs of objects.	– Which of these two containers can hold [more/less]? – What else can you tell me about these two containers?	Can the pupil compare the capacities of two containers?
Pointing to one of the containers, ask the pupil questions similar to the ones shown here: Repeat for other objects.	– Point to a container that can hold [more than/less than] this container. – Which containers can hold [more than/less than] this container?	Can the pupil compare the capacity of one container to the capacities of several other containers? Does the pupil understand the language associated with capacity?

Success criterion E: Compare volumes by direct comparison using appropriate language

What to do	What to say	What to look out for
Place the four identical containers in front of the pupil.		
Ask the pupil questions similar to the ones shown here:	– *Which of these containers has the most amount of water in it?* – *Which container is full?* – *Which container is half-full?* – *Which container is empty?*	Can the pupil compare the volumes of different containers? Does the pupil understand the language associated with volume?

Success criterion F: Compare time using appropriate language

What to do	What to say	What to look out for

Ask the pupil questions similar to the ones shown here. Questions should aim to elicit an assessment of the pupil's understanding of the following language:
  – before, after
  – next, last
  – now, soon
  – early, earlier
  – late, later
  – quick, quicker, quickest, quickly
  – fast, faster, fastest
  – slow, slower, slowest, slowly
  – old, older, oldest
  – new, newer, newest
  – takes longer, takes less time
	– *What are we doing now?*
	– *Tell me something you did before we sat down to do this.*
	– *Tell me something you did earlier today.*
	– *What is something you might do [after/next/later]?*
	– *Tell me something you might do later today.*
	– *Which is slower: walking or running?*
	– *Which animal can move faster: a cat or a snail?*
	– *Do you have an older brother or sister? How old are they?*
	– *Can you tell me something that's old?*
	– *Which is longer: playtime or lunchtime?*
		Does the pupil understand and use appropriate language to describe time?

What to do for those pupils working *below* or *above* expectations

Refer to the 'Tracking back and forward through the Mathematics National Curriculum attainment targets' charts on pages 193–200.

Measurement

National Curriculum attainment target

- Measure and begin to record the following:
  - lengths and heights
  - mass/weight
  - capacity and volume
  - time (hours, minutes, seconds)

Prerequisite checklist

Can the pupil:

- compare, order and describe two or three items by length or height?
- compare, order and describe two or three items by weight?
- compare, order and describe two or three items by capacity?
- use everyday language related to time?
- measure short periods of time in simple ways?

Success criteria

A. Measure the lengths of objects, choosing and using suitable uniform non-standard or standard units and measuring instruments, and recording such measurements

B. Measure the heights of objects, choosing and using suitable uniform non-standard or standard units and measuring instruments, and recording such measurements

C. Weigh the masses of objects, choosing and using suitable uniform non-standard or standard units and measuring instruments, and recording such measurements

D. Measure the capacity of containers, choosing and using suitable uniform non-standard or standard units and measuring instruments, and recording such measurements

E. Measure the volume of containers, choosing and using suitable uniform non-standard or standard units and measuring instruments, and recording such measurements

F. Estimate and measure time

Resources

- pencil and paper (per pupil)

Length and height:
- about 6 objects measuring from 10 cm to 1 m (ensure that the objects can be used to describe length and/or height)
- selection of uniform non-standard measures, e.g. counters, cubes and matchsticks
- 30 cm ruler
- metre stick marked in centimetres

Mass/weight:
- about 6 objects weighing from 1 kg to 2 kg
- balance
- selection of uniform non-standard measures, e.g. marbles
- 1 kg and 2 kg weights
- weighting scales

Capacity:
- about 6 empty containers of different shapes and sizes from 250 ml to 2 litres
- bucket of water
- selection of uniform non-standard measures, e.g. cup, yoghurt pot, spoon
- 1 litre measuring jug

Volume:
- 3 identical containers: one full of water, one half-full of water, and one about one quarter-full of water
- selection of uniform non-standard measures, e.g. cup, yoghurt pot, spoon
- 1 litre measuring jug

Time:
- pencil and paper
- container holding a large number of tiny objects, e.g. small counters or beads
- reading book suitable to the age and ability of the pupil

NOTES

- The selection of uniform non-standard measures is designed to provide pupils with a choice when measuring different lengths, heights, masses, capacities and volumes. It is assumed that those pupils who choose to use suitable standard equipment such as a ruler, a metre stick, a balance, weights and a measuring jug, as well as standard units such as metres, centimetres, kilograms and litres, will be working at a higher level than those pupils who choose to use uniform non-standard units.

- Given the difference between the four measures assessed in this Assessment Task, i.e. length and height, mass/weight, capacity and volume, and time, it is recommended that each measure is assessed seperately, at a different time.

Assessment Task

Success criterion A: Measure the lengths of objects, choosing and using suitable uniform non-standard or standard units and measuring instruments, and recording such measurements

What to do	What to say	What to look out for
Place the objects of different lengths and heights in front of the pupil along with the selection of uniform non-standard measures, the ruler and the metre stick.		
Pointing to one of the objects that clearly shows length, ask the pupil questions similar to the ones shown here:	– How could you find out how long the [...] is? – What could you use to measure it? – What units of measure [would be suitable/would not be suitable] for measuring it?	As the pupil works on the task assess the following: – whether they use uniform non-standard or standard measuring equipment to measure length – whether they use uniform non-standard or standard units to measure length – their ability to measure a length – how they record the measurement.
Ask the pupil to find the length of the object.	Measure the length of the [...].	
Give the pupil pencil and paper and ask them to record the length of the object.	How would you write down the length of this [...]?	
Repeat for other objects.		

NOTE If the pupil uses standard measuring equipment and units to measure an object, given that the objects the pupil is measuring will more than likely not measure a whole number of centimetres or metres, the pupil is not expected to measure or record an object to the nearest millimetre or metres and centimetres. Describing an object as 'more than/less than/about 10 centimetres' is sufficient at this stage.

Success criterion B: Measure the heights of objects, choosing and using suitable uniform non-standard or standard units and measuring instruments, and recording such measurements

What to do	What to say	What to look out for
Pointing to one of the objects that clearly shows height, ask the pupil questions similar to the ones shown here:	– How could you find out how tall the [...] is? – What could you use to measure it? – What units of measure [would be suitable/would not be suitable for measuring it]?	As the pupil works on the task assess the following: – whether they use uniform non-standard or standard measuring equipment to measure height – whether they use uniform non-standard or standard units to measure height – their ability to measure a height – how they record the measurement.
Ask the pupil to find the height of the object.	Measure the height of the [...]	
Give the pupil pencil and paper and ask them to record the height of the object.	How would you write down the height of the [...]?	
Repeat for other objects.		

NOTE If the pupil uses standard measuring equipment and units to measure an object, given that the objects the pupil is measuring will more than likely not measure a whole number of centimetres or metres, the pupil is not expected to measure or record an object to the nearest millimetre or metres and centimetres. Describing an object as 'more than/less than/about 10 centimetres' is sufficient at this stage.

Success criterion C: Weigh the masses of objects, choosing and using suitable uniform non-standard or standard units and measuring instruments, and recording such measurements

What to do	What to say	What to look out for
Place the objects of different masses/weights in front of the pupil along with the balance, the selection of uniform non-standard measures, the 1 kg and 2 kg weights and the weighing scales.		
Pointing to one of the objects, ask the pupil questions similar to the ones shown here:	– *How could you find out how heavy it is?* – *What could you use to find out how heavy it is?* – *What units of measure [would be suitable/would not be suitable] for weighing it?*	As the pupil works on the task assess the following: – whether they use uniform non-standard or standard measuring equipment to weigh a mass – whether they use uniform non-standard or standard units to weigh a mass – their ability to weigh a mass – how they record the measurement.
Ask the pupil to find the mass of the object.	*Measure how heavy the […] is.*	
Give the pupil pencil and paper and ask them to record the mass of the object.	*How would you write down how heavy the […] is?*	
Repeat for other objects.		

NOTE If the pupil uses standard measuring equipment and units to weigh an object, given that the objects the pupil is weighing will more than likely not weigh a whole number of kilograms, the pupil is not expected to weigh or record an object to the nearest gram. Describing an object as 'more than/less than/about half a kilogram' is sufficient at this stage.

Success criterion D: Measure the capacity of containers, choosing and using suitable uniform non-standard or standard units and measuring instruments, and recording such measurements

What to do	What to say	What to look out for
Place the empty containers of different shapes and sizes in front of the pupil along with the bucket of water, the non-standard measures and the 1 litre measuring jug.		
Pointing to one of the containers, ask the pupil questions similar to the ones shown here:	– *How could you find out how much it can hold?* – *What could you use to find out?* – *What units of measure [would be suitable/would not be suitable] for finding out how much it can hold?*	As the pupil works on the task assess the following: – whether they use non-standard or standard measuring equipment to measure capacity – whether they use non-standard or standard units to measure capacity – their ability to measure a capacity – how they record the measurement.
Ask the pupil to find the capacity of the container.	*Measure how much this container can hold.*	
Give the pupil pencil and paper and ask them to record the capacity of the container.	*How would you write down how much it can hold?*	
Repeat for other containers.		
Place the empty containers of different shapes and sizes and the bucket of water to one side.		

NOTE If the pupil uses standard measuring equipment and units to measure a capacity, given that the containers the pupil is using will more than likely not hold a whole number of litres, the pupil is not expected to measure or record the capacity of a container to the nearest millilitre. Describing a container as 'more than/less than/about half a litre' is sufficient at this stage.

Success criterion E: Measure the volume of containers, choosing and using suitable uniform non-standard or standard units and measuring instruments, and recording such measurements

What to do	What to say	What to look out for
Place the three identical containers in front of the pupil. Ensure that the pupil still has access to the non-standard measures and the 1 litre measuring jug.		
Pointing to one of the containers, ask the pupil questions similar to the ones shown here:	– *How could you find out how much water is in this container?* – *What could you use to find out?* – *What units of measure [would be suitable/would not be suitable] for finding out how much water is in this container?*	As the pupil works on the task assess the following: – whether they use non-standard or standard measuring equipment to measure volume – whether they use non-standard or standard units to measure volume – their ability to measure a volume – how they record the measurement.
Ask the pupil to find the volume of the container.	*Measure how much water is in this container.*	
Give the pupil pencil and paper and ask them to record the volume of the container.	*How would you write down how much water is in this container?*	
Repeat for other containers.		

NOTE If the pupil uses standard measuring equipment and units to measure a volume, given that the containers the pupil is using will more than likely not hold a whole number of litres, the pupil is not expected to measure or record the volume of a container to the nearest millilitre. Describing a container as 'more than/less than/about half a litre' is sufficient at this stage.

Success criterion F: Estimate and measure time

What to do	What to say	What to look out for
Ask the pupil questions similar to the ones shown here. Questions should aim to elicit an assessment of the pupil's ability to estimate and measure time using the following terms: – year – month – week – day – hour – minute – second.	– *Would you go on holiday for a minute? What about an hour?* – *How long might you go on holiday for?* – *When we do PE, does it last for about a second, a minute or an hour?* – *For about how many hours do you come to school each day?* – *How long would it take us to walk to the school gate and back?* – *What's your favourite TV show? How long does it last?*	Does the pupil understand and use appropriate language to estimate and measure time?
Write the pupil's name on a piece of paper.	*How long do you think it took me to write your name?*	
Show the pupil the container holding a large number of tiny objects.	*How long do you think it would take me to count all of these […]?*	
Show the pupil the reading book.	*How long do you think it would take you to read this book?*	

NOTE To assess a pupil's ability to record time, refer to Assessment Task(s) 17 and/or 18.

What to do for those pupils working *below* or *above* expectations

Refer to the 'Tracking back and forward through the Mathematics National Curriculum attainment targets' charts on pages 193–200.

Measurement

National Curriculum attainment target

- Recognise and know the value of different denominations of coins and notes

Prerequisite checklist

Can the pupil:
- use everyday language related to money?

Success criteria

A. Recognise different denominations of coins and notes
B. Know the value of different denominations of coins and notes

Resources

container holding 20 × 1 p coins
container holding 10 × 2 p coins
container holding 4 × 5 p coins
container holding 2 × 10 p coins
one each of the following coins and notes: 20 p, 50 p, £1, £2, £5, £10 (if easily available: £20 and £50)
Alternatively, use several copies of Resource 20: Coins and notes

NOTE

- It is recommended that if possible real coins (and notes) are used for this Assessment Task. If this is not possible, then use realistic plastic coins and notes. Only as a final alternative use the coins and notes provided on Resource 20.

Assessment Task

Success criterion A: Recognise different denominations of coins and notes

What to do	What to say	What to look out for
Place one each of the following coins and notes in front of the pupil: 1 p, 2 p, 5 p, 10 p, 20 p, 50 p, £1, £2, £5, £10 (and, if available, £20 and £50).		
Ask questions similar to the ones shown here that require the pupil to recognise each of the coins and notes.	– *Point to the 20 p coin.* – *Hand me the £10 note.* – *What is this [coin/note]?*	Does the pupil recognise each coin and note?

Success criterion B: Know the value of different denominations of coins and notes

What to do	What to say	What to look out for
Alongside the 1 p, 2 p, 5 p, 10 p, 20 p, 50 p, £1, £2, £5, £10 (and if available £20 and £50), place the four containers of 1 p, 2 p, 5 p and 10 p coins in front of the pupil.		
Ask questions similar to the ones shown here that require the pupil to demonstrate that they know the value of different denominations of coins, e.g. $2\,p = 2 \times 1\,p$ coins $5\,p = 5 \times 1\,p$ coin $10\,p = 2 \times 5\,p$ coin $\quad\quad = 5 \times 2\,p$ coins $\quad\quad = 10 \times 1\,p$ coins $20\,p = 2 \times 10\,p$ coins $\quad\quad = 4 \times 5\,p$ coins $\quad\quad = 10 \times 2\,p$ coins $\quad\quad = 20 \times 1\,p$ coins. Encourage the pupil to use the coins to demonstrate the equivalences.	– *Look at this 2 p coin. How many 1 p coins would you need to make 2 pence?* – *Look at this 5 p coin. How could you make 5 pence using just penny pieces?* – *Take this 10 p coin. How could you make 10 pence using just 1 pence pieces?* – *Could you make 10 p just using 2 pence pieces? What about making 10 p using just 5 pence pieces?* – *Here is a 20 pence piece. Can you use these 1 p coins to make 20 pence?* – *Can you use these 2 p coins to make 20 pence?* – *What about using the 5 p coins to make 20 pence?* – *How many 10 p coins would you need to make 20 pence?*	Does the pupil know the value of the 2 p, 5 p, 10 p and 20 p coins and are they able to demonstrate this in different ways?
If appropriate, ask questions similar to the ones shown here that require the pupil to demonstrate that they know the value of the 50 p, £1 and £2 coins, and the £5, £10 (and, if available, £20 and £50).	– *How many 1 p coins would you need to make the same value as this 50 p coin?* – *How many 1 p coins make £1?* – *How many 10 p coins make £1?* – *Look at this £2 coin. How many £1 coins total the same value as the £2 coin?* – *How many £1 coins is the same amount as a £5 note?* – *How many £1 coins would you need to make £10?* – *A £20 note has the same value as how many £1 coins?* – *If I had £50, how many £1 coins would you need so that you had the same amount of money?*	Does the pupil know the value of the 50 p, £1 and £2 coins and are they able to demonstrate this in different ways? Does the pupil know the value of the £5, £10, £20 and £50 notes and are they able to demonstrate this in different ways?

What to do for those pupils working *below* or *above* expectations

Refer to the 'Tracking back and forward through the Mathematics National Curriculum attainment targets' charts on pages 193–200.

Measurement

National Curriculum attainment target

- Sequence events in chronological order using language [for example, before and after, next, first, today, yesterday, tomorrow, morning, afternoon and evening]

Prerequisite checklist

Can the pupil:
- use everyday language related to time?
- order and sequence familiar events?
- measure short periods of time in a simple way?

Success criteria

A. Understand the language related to time, including times of the day (e.g. today, yesterday, tomorrow, morning, afternoon and evening, night)
B. Sequence a familiar event in chronological order
C. Sequence events in chronological order

Resources

Resource 21: Sequencing events (1)
Resource 22: Sequencing events (2)

NOTES

- Resource 21 involves the pupil sequencing eight events in chronological order and Resource 22 involves the pupil sequencing six events. Success criterion C begins with using Resource 21 (eight events). If appropriate, change the order of using the Resources so that the task begins with Resource 22 and the pupil sequencing just six events.
- For Resource 22, there is more than one logical sequence of events. The picture that shows the family in the car park at the beach could either show them arriving at the beach or leaving the beach.
- Prior to the Assessment Task, ensure that the cards from Resource 21 and Resource 22 are not in chronological order.

Assessment Task

Success criterion A: Understand the language related to time, including times of the day (e.g. today, yesterday, tomorrow, morning, afternoon and evening, night)

What to do	What to say	What to look out for
Ask questions similar to the ones shown here that require the pupil to use the language related to time.	– What day is it today? – Tell me something we did earlier this morning. – What day was it yesterday? – Can you remember something we did in class yesterday? – What is something you might do this afternoon when you get home from school? – Tell me something you will do [this evening/tonight]? – What day is it tomorrow? – What is something that [you/we] usually do on a […]?	Does the pupil understand the terms today, yesterday, tomorrow? Does the pupil understand the language related to the different time periods in a day?

Success criterion B: Sequence a familiar event in chronological order

What to do	What to say	What to look out for

Ask the pupil to describe the sequence of events for one or more of the following scenarios:
  – the things they do in the morning before they come to school
  – their day at school
  – what they do in the afternoon/evening after school.
	Tell me what you did this morning before you came to school. Try to tell me what you did in the order in which you did them. So you began by waking up and getting out of bed. Then what did you do? What did you do next? Then what did you do?	Can the pupil sequence a familiar event?

Repeat above for other scenarios until the pupil has sufficiently demonstrated that they can sequence a familiar event in chronological order.

Success criterion C: Sequence events in chronological order

What to do	What to say	What to look out for
Place the cards from Resource 21 in front of the pupil.		
Briefly discuss with the pupil the idea of redecorating a bedroom. Explain to the pupil that the scenes on the cards show the sequence of some of the events that were involved in redecorating a girl's bedroom. However, all of the pictures are not in the correct order.	*These cards show what happened when Julia had her bedroom redecorated. However, the cards are in not in the right order.*	
Ask the pupil to arrange the cards to show a logical sequence of events.	*Can you put these cards in the order in which you think Julia and her mother redecorated her room?* *Which card do you think comes first?* *Then what might have happened next?*	Can the pupil sequence the events in a logical order?
Once the pupil has placed the cards in a logical sequence, ask them to go through the sequence of pictures and briefly explain to you what happened.	*Now let's have a look at these eight cards. Starting with the first card tell me what happened.*	
Tell the pupil to close their eyes. Change the order of two or more of the cards.	*Open your eyes. I have moved some of these cards around so now the order in which Julia and her mum redecorated her room doesn't make any sense.* *Can you fix what I have done so that it makes sense?*	Does the pupil recognise when events are out of sequence? Can they sequence the events back into a logical order?

If necessary repeat above, using the cards from Resource 22, until the pupil has sufficiently demonstrated that they can sequence events in chronological order.

What to do for those pupils working *below* or *above* expectations

Refer to the 'Tracking back and forward through the Mathematics National Curriculum attainment targets' charts on pages 193–200.

Measurement

National Curriculum attainment target

• Recognise and use language relating to dates, including days of the week, weeks, months and years

Prerequisite checklist

Can the pupil:
• use everyday language related to time?
• order and sequence familiar events?
• measure short periods of time in simple ways?

Success criteria

A. Use the language related to the days of the week, and order days of the week
B. Use the language related to the months of the year, and order months of the year
C. Use the language related to the seasons of the year, and order seasons of the year
D. Use the language related to dates

Resources

Resource 23: Time
current year's calendar
pencil and paper (optional)

Assessment Task

Success criterion A: Use the language related to the days of the week, and order days of the week

What to do	What to say	What to look out for
Ask questions similar to the ones shown here that require the pupil to use the language related to the days of the week.	– What day is it today? So what will tomorrow be? – How many days are there in a week? – Which are the weekend days? – Which days are we at school?	Can the pupil use the language related to the days of the week?
Spread the days of the week cards from Resource 23 face up on the table in front of the pupil. Point to two or three cards in turn.	What day of the week does this card show? What day of the week is this?	Can the pupil read the days of the week?
	Point to the card that says 'Saturday'. Which card reads 'Tuesday'?	
Take the card that reads 'Monday' and place it to the extreme left of the pupil.	Hand me the card that shows the day of the week that comes after Monday.	Can the pupil order the days of the week?
Place the 'Tuesday' card to the right of the 'Monday' card.	Which day of the week comes after Tuesday?	
Repeat above until all the days of the week cards are in order.		
Collect the days of the week cards and place them to one side.		

Success criterion B: Use the language related to the months of the year, and order months of the year

What to do	What to say	What to look out for
Ask questions similar to the ones shown here that require the pupil to use the language related to the months of the year.	– How many months are there in one year? – What month is your birthday in? – Which month comes after March? – Which month comes before September?	Can the pupil use the language related to the months of the year?

What to do	What to say	What to look out for
Spread the months of the year cards from Resource 23 face up on the table in front of the pupil. Point to two or three cards in turn.	*What month does this card show?* *What month is this?*	Can the pupil read the months of the year?
	Point to the card that says 'June'. *Which card reads 'October'?*	
Take the card that reads 'January' and place it to the extreme left of the pupil.	*Will you pass me the card that shows the month that comes after January?*	Can the pupil order the months of the year?
Place the 'February' card to the right of the 'January' card.	*Which month comes after February?*	
Repeat above until all the months of the year cards are in order.		
Leave the months of the year cards in order on the table for Success criterion D.		

Success criterion C: Use the language related to the seasons of the year, and order seasons of the year

What to do	What to say	What to look out for
Ask questions similar to the ones shown here that require the pupil to use the language related to the seasons of the year.	– *How many seasons are there?* – *What season is it now?* – *When it's your birthday, what season is it?* – *In which season do the leaves fall off the trees?*	Can the pupil use the language related to the seasons of the year?
Ask questions that require the pupil to order the seasons of the year.	– *Which season comes after spring?* – *Which season comes before winter?* – *Which season comes after autumn?* – *Which season comes before summer?*	Can the pupil order the seasons of the year?

Success criterion D: Use the language related to dates

What to do	What to say	What to look out for
Place the current years calendar in front of the pupil near the ordered months of the year cards. Ask questions similar to the ones shown here that require the pupil to use the language related to dates. At this stage, pupils are not expected to be able to read and interpret a calendar, so if the pupil is unfamiliar with calendars, assist them in reading it. The calendar is only used in this task as a means of helping the pupil to know today's date. If appropriate, use pencil and paper to record the information the pupil tells you about today's date.	– *Look at this calendar; it helps us to keep track of what month it is and what day in the month it is.* – *What year is it?* – *What month is it?* – *If January is the first month of the year, and December is the 12th month of the year, what month is […]?* – *What day is it today?* – *Do you know what day in the month it is?* (If the pupil does not know this, show and tell them the day of the month on the calendar.) – *Can you tell me what today's date is?*	Can the pupil demonstrate an understanding of the language related to dates? Can the pupil demonstrate some understanding of how to say today's date?

What to do for those pupils working *below* or *above* expectations

Refer to the 'Tracking back and forward through the Mathematics National Curriculum attainment targets' charts on pages 193–200.

Measurement

National Curriculum attainment target

• Tell the time to the hour and half past the hour and draw the hands on a clock face to show these times

Prerequisite checklist

Can the pupil:

• use everyday language related to time?
• measure periods of time in simple ways, including hours?
• demonstrate an understanding of o'clock?

Success criteria

A. Read the time to the hour on an analogue clock
B. Show the time to the hour on an analogue clock
C. Read the time to the half-hour on an analogue clock
D. Show the time to the half-hour on an analogue clock

Resources

• demonstration analogue clock

Assessment Task

Success criterion A: Read the time to the hour on an analogue clock

What to do	What to say	What to look out for
Show a time to the hour on the analogue clock, e.g. 7:00.	*What time does this clock show?*	Can the pupil read the time to the hour?

Repeat several times until the pupil has sufficiently demonstrated their ability to read the time to the hour on an analogue clock.

Success criterion B: Show the time to the hour on an analogue clock

What to do	What to say	What to look out for
Place the analogue clock in front of the pupil.	*What would ten o'clock look like on this clock?*	Can the pupil show the time to the hour, placing both hands in the correct position?

Repeat several times until the pupil has sufficiently demonstrated their ability to show the time to the hour on an analogue clock.

Success criterion C: Read the time to the half-hour on an analogue clock

What to do	What to say	What to look out for
Show a time to the half-hour on the analogue clock, e.g. 4:30.	*What time does this clock show?* (e.g. 'four thirty') *How else can you say this time?* (e.g. 'half past four')	Can the pupil read the time to the half-hour?

Repeat several times until the pupil has sufficiently demonstrated their ability to read the time to the half-hour on an analogue clock.

Success criterion D: Show the time to the half-hour on an analogue clock

What to do	What to say	What to look out for
Place the analogue clock in front of the pupil.	*Show me half past eight on this clock.*	Can the pupil show the time to the half-hour, placing both hands in the correct position (i.e. the hour hand half-way between the previous and next o'clock times)?

Repeat several times until the pupil has sufficiently demonstrated their ability to show the time to the half-hour on an analogue clock.

What to do for those pupils working *below* or *above* expectations

Refer to the 'Tracking back and forward through the Mathematics National Curriculum attainment targets' charts on pages 193–200.

Geometry – Properties of shapes

National Curriculum attainment target

- Recognise and name common 2-D and 3-D shapes, including:
  - 2-D shapes [for example, rectangles (including squares), circles and triangles]
  - 3-D shapes [for example, cuboids (including cubes), pyramids and spheres]

Prerequisite checklist

Can the pupil:

- use the mathematical names for 2-D 'flat' shapes and 3-D 'solid' shapes?
- select a particular named shape?
- describe 2-D and 3-D shapes?

Success criteria

A. Recognise and name common 2-D shapes
B. Visualise and name common 2-D shapes
C. Recognise and name common 3-D shapes
D. Visualise and name common 3-D shapes

Resources

set of the following regular 2-D shapes: circles, triangles, squares, rectangles (include several of the same shape in different sizes as well as different types of triangles)

set of the following 3-D shapes: cube, cuboid, square-based pyramid and/or triangular-based pyramid, sphere, cone, cylinder

the following 'real-life' objects (or similar): 1–6 die, cereal box, pyramid-shaped sweet box, tennis ball, sports cone, can of drink

NOTE

- At this stage pupils are not expected to differentiate between a square-based pyramid and a triangular-based pyramid (tetrahedron). Being able to recognise both as being a 'pyramid' is sufficient at this stage.

Assessment Task

Success criterion A: Recognise and name common 2-D shapes

What to do	What to say	What to look out for
Place the 2-D shapes on the table in front of the pupil.		
Pointing to one of the 2-D shapes, ask the pupil to name the shape.	*What is this shape called?*	Can the pupil recognise and name all of the 2-D shapes?
Repeat above for each of the 2-D shapes. Include statements that require the pupil to identify a named 2-D shape.	*Point to a triangle.*	

Success criterion B: Visualise and name common 2-D shapes

What to do	What to say	What to look out for
Describe one of the 2-D shapes to the pupil.	*I'm thinking of a shape. It has four sides. The opposite sides of this shape are the same length. What shape am I thinking of?*	Can the pupil visualise and name all of the 2-D shapes?
Repeat above until the pupil has named all four shapes.		
Place the 2-D shapes to one side.		

Success criterion C: Recognise and name common 3-D shapes

What to do	What to say	What to look out for
Place the six or seven 3-D shapes on the table in front of the pupil.		
Pointing to one of the 3-D shapes, ask the pupil to name the shape.	*What shape is this?*	Can the pupil recognise and name all of the 3-D shapes?
Repeat above for each of the 3-D shapes. Include statements that require the pupil to identify a named 3-D shape.	*Point to the cone.*	
Place the 'real-life' objects with the 3-D shapes.		
Repeat above, pointing to each of the 'real-life' objects.	*What shape is this dice?*	Can the pupil recognise and name 'real-life' examples of 3-D shapes in different orientations?

Success criterion D: Visualise and name common 3-D shapes

What to do	What to say	What to look out for
Describe one of the 3-D shapes to the pupil.	*I'm thinking of a shape. It has eight corners. What shape am I thinking of? Is there another shape with eight corners? What do we call this shape?*	Can the pupil visualise and name all of the 3-D shapes?
Repeat above until the pupil has named all of the 3-D shapes.		

What to do for those pupils working *below* or *above* expectations

Refer to the 'Tracking back and forward through the Mathematics National Curriculum attainment targets' charts on pages 193–200.

Geometry – Position and direction

National Curriculum attainment target

- Describe position, direction and movement, including whole, half, quarter and three-quarter turns

Prerequisite checklist

Can the pupil:
- describe their relative position such as 'behind' or 'next to'?

Success criteria

A. Visualise and use everyday language to describe the position of objects

B. Visualise and use everyday language to describe direction and distance

C. Identify objects that turn about a point or about a line

D. Recognise and make whole, half, quarter and three-quarter turns

Resources

Resource 24: Position and direction (enlarged to A3)

pencil and paper clip (for the spinner)

button, or similar playing piece (per pupil and yourself)

pile of counters

selection of objects that turn about a point, e.g. scissors, analogue clock, handheld windmill, pair of compasses

selection of objects that turn about a line, e.g. book, hinged box, cereal packet

selection of objects that do not turn, e.g. pencil, eraser, ball, shoe

Resource 25: Turns (enlarged to A3)

Compare Bear (or similar)

NOTE

- This attainment target involves quite different concepts: position, direction and movement. The Success criteria for this Assessment Task reflects these differences. Given this, and the fact that all four Success criteria will take some time to assess, it is advisable to choose just two Success criteria at a time. It is recommended that Success criteria A and B, involving position and direction, are assessed together, and that Success criteria C and D, which involve movement, are assessed together on a separate occasion.

Assessment Task

Success criterion A: Visualise and use everyday language to describe the position of objects

What to do	What to say	What to look out for
Place Resource 24 on the table in front of the pupil. If the task is being undertaken with more than one pupil, then ensure that each pupil is viewing the Resource from the same perspective.		

What to do	What to say	What to look out for
Briefly discuss any of the illustrations the pupil may not recognise. Tell the pupil to ignore for the moment the black boxes and the 'Start' box. Pointing to the objects on the grid, ask questions similar to the ones shown here:	–*Tell me something that is next to the [...]* –*Tell me something that is to the right of the [...]* –*Tell me something that is higher than the [...]* –*What is next to the [...]?* –*Point to something that is on the edge of the grid.* –*What is below the [...]?* –*Point to something that is higher than the [...]* –*What is between the [...] and the [...]?* –*Tell me something that is higher than the [...] and lower than the [...].* –*What is to the right of the [...]?* –*Tell me something that is towards the middle of the sheet.*	Does the pupil understand everyday language to describe the position of objects?
Ask the pupil to choose two objects on the grid and describe their position in relation to each other.	*Point to two objects on the grid. Good. What can you tell me about the position of these two objects?*	Can the pupil use everyday language to describe the position of objects?

Repeat above until the pupil has sufficiently demonstrated that they can visualise and use everyday language to describe the position of objects.

Success criterion B: Visualise and use everyday language to describe direction and distance

What to do	What to say	What to look out for
With Resource 24 still on the table, ask the pupil questions similar to the ones shown here:	– *Find the tennis racket. Describe to me how you would get from the tennis racket to the banana.* – *If the rabbit wanted to eat the carrot, which direction would he need to move? How many squares would he need to jump?*	Can the pupil use everyday language to describe direction and distance?

What to do

Place the pencil, paper clip, buttons (or similar playing pieces) and pile of counters beside the Resource 24.

Discuss with the pupil the directions on the spinner.

If you are undertaking this task with more than one pupil, then provide each pupil with a different button. If you are doing the task with only one pupil, then give the pupil and yourself a different button.

Explain to the pupil that you are going to play a game together.

Explain the rules of the game to the pupil:

- Everyone places their button on 'Start'.
- They take turns to spin the spinner, e.g. 2 up, and move their button accordingly.
- If a player lands on a black box that shows 1, 2 or 3 stars, then they collect a counter for each star.
- If the position of a player's button is towards the top, bottom, left or right of the grid and on their next turn the direction on the spinner means they will go off the grid, then they spin the spinner again.
- The game continues in this way.
- The winner is the first player to collect 10 counters or the player with the most counters after a predetermined time.

How to use the spinner

Hold the paper clip in the centre of the spinner using the pencil and gently flick the paper clip with your finger to make it spin

What to say

Find the tennis racket. Describe to me how you would get from the tennis racket to the banana.
If the rabbit wanted to eat the carrot, in which direction would he need to move? How many squares would he need to jump?

What to look out for

Can the pupil use everyday language to describe direction and distance?
As the pupil plays the game, assess their ability to visualise and use everyday language to describe direction and distance.

Success criterion C: Identify objects that turn about a point or about a line

What to do	What to say	What to look out for
Place the selection of objects that turn about a point or about a line and those objects that do not turn on the table in front of the pupil.		
Ask the pupil to describe the objects using their own criteria.	*What can you tell me about these objects? Can you sort them in any way?*	Can the pupil sort the objects into two groups: – those objects that can turn about a point or a line; – those objects that cannot?
Then ask the pupil to choose an object that: – turns – does not turn.	*Point to an object that has a part of it that turns. Where does it turn?*	Can the pupil identify an object that turns? Can the pupil identify an object that turns about a point?
Ask the pupil to suggest other objects that turn about a point or a line. If these objects are in the classroom, e.g. door handle, window, cupboard or tap. Ask them to show how they turn.	*Can you find something else in this room that has a part of it that can turn? Can you tell me something else that has a part of it that can turn?*	Can the pupil identify an object that turns about a line?
Place the selection of objects to one side.		

Success criterion D: Recognise and make whole, half, quarter and three-quarter turns

What to do	What to say	What to look out for
Place Resource 25 on the table in front of the pupil. If the task is being undertaken with more than one pupil, then ensure that each pupil is viewing the Resource from the same perspective.		
Place the Compare Bear (or similar) on the island facing the forest.	*What is the Compare Bear looking at?* (forest)	
Briefly discuss the scene with the pupil and ensure that they know what each of the illustrations is.		
Turn the Compare Bear through half a turn.	*The Compare Bear was looking at the forest. He made half a turn and now he is looking at the restaurant and shop.*	
Turn the Compare Bear one quarter turn to the right.	*Now the Compare Bear is looking at the picnic area. In which direction did he turn? How much of a turn did he make?*	Does the pupil recognise the movement as one quarter turn? Does the pupil recognise the movement as one quarter turn to the right?
Repeat above several times turning the Compare Bear through whole, half, quarter and three-quarter turns and asking the pupil to a say the direction and amount of turn you moved the Compare Bear.	*Now the Compare Bear is looking at the [...]. How much of a turn did he make? In which direction did he turn?*	Can the pupil describe the amount of turn, i.e. – whole turn – half turn – quarter turn – three-quarter turn? Can the pupil describe the direction of the turn, i.e. – to the left – to the right?

What to do	What to say	What to look out for
Next, place the Compare Bear so that it is once again facing the forest.		
Ask the pupil to move the Compare Bear through half a turn.	*I want you to show me what the bear would face if he made half a turn.*	Can the pupil make a: – whole turn? – half turn?
Repeat above, asking the pupil to move the Compare Bear through a whole turn, one half turn, one quarter turn to the right or to the left, or a three-quarter turn to the right or to the left.	*Can you move the Compare Bear to show me what he would be facing if he made a three-quarter turn to his left?* *What if the bear then made one quarter turn to the right? What would he be looking at?*	– quarter turn to the right? – quarter turn to the left? – three-quarter turn to the right? – three-quarter turn to the left?

What to do for those pupils working *below* or *above* expectations

Refer to the 'Tracking back and forward through the Mathematics National Curriculum attainment targets' charts on pages 193–200.

Domain: _____

National Curriculum attainment target (NC AT): _____

_____

Teacher: _____ Class: _____ Date: _____

	Success criteria	Name												
A														
B														
C														
D														
E														
F														
Other observations														
Level of mastery of NC AT*		NYA	A	A&E	NYA	A	A&E	NYA	A	A&E	NYA	A	A&E	
Future action														

Level of mastery key: NYA – Not yet achieved | A – Achieved | A&E – Achieved and exceeded

Name: _____ **Date:** _____

Number and place value

Continue to count. What numbers come next?

1 | 0 | 1 | 2 | 3 | 4 | ☐ ☐ ☐ ☐ ☐ ☐   1   1 mark

2 | 10 | 9 | 8 | 7 | 6 | ☐ ☐ ☐ ☐ ☐ ☐   2   1 mark

3 | 1 | 2 | 3 | 4 | 5 | ☐ ☐ ☐ ☐ ☐ ☐ ☐   3   1 mark

4 | 16 | 17 | 18 | 19 | 20 | ☐ ☐ ☐ ☐ ☐ ☐ ☐   4   1 mark

5 | 20 | 19 | 18 | 17 | 16 | ☐ ☐ ☐ ☐ ☐ ☐ ☐   5   1 mark

6 | 53 | 54 | 55 | 56 | 57 | ☐ ☐ ☐ ☐ ☐ ☐ ☐   6   1 mark

7 | 46 | 45 | 44 | 43 | 42 | ☐ ☐ ☐ ☐ ☐ ☐ ☐   7   1 mark

8 | 85 | 86 | 87 | 88 | 89 | ☐ ☐ ☐ ☐ ☐ ☐ ☐   8   1 mark

9 | 77 | 76 | 75 | 74 | 73 | ☐ ☐ ☐ ☐ ☐ ☐ ☐   9   1 mark

10 | 93 | 94 | 95 | 96 | 97 | ☐ ☐ ☐ ☐ ☐ ☐ ☐   10   1 mark

● count to and across 100, forwards and backwards, beginning with 0 or 1, or from any given number

Total: ☐ out of 10   Mastery: NYA | A | A&E

Name: _____   Date: _____

Number and place value

1 2   4   6   8

1 mark   **1**

2 10   20   30   40

1 mark   **2**

3 5   10   15   20

1 mark   **3**

4 30   40   70   100

1 mark   **4**

5 45   50   55   70

1 mark   **5**

6 22   24   28   34

1 mark   **6**

7 How many carrots?

1 mark   **7**

8 How much money? Count in twos.

1 mark   **8**

9 How many sweets? Count in tens.

1 mark   **9**

10 How many pens? Count in fives.

1 mark   **10**

● count, read and write numbers to 100 in numerals; count in multiples of twos, fives and tens

Total: ☐ out of 10   Mastery: NYA   A   A&E

Name: _____ Date: _____

Number and place value

1 Write the number that is **1 more**.

a)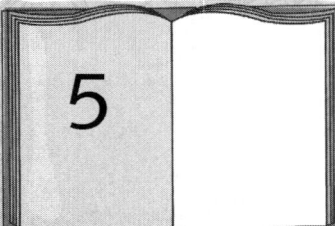

b)

c)

d)

e)

1
5 marks

2 Write the number that is **1 less**.

a)

b)

c)

d)

e)

2
5 marks

● given a number, identify one more and one less   Total: [ ] out of 10   Mastery: NYA | A | A&E

Name: _____   Date: _____

Number and place value

1 Circle 12 gloves.

1
1 mark

2 Circle the tray that is holding **more** fruit.

2
1 mark

3 Circle the necklace with **fewer** beads.

3
1 mark

4 a) Circle the number that is **less**.   b) Circle the number that is **more**.

| 7 | 18 | | 11 | 15 |

4
2 marks

5 Circle the 2 leaves that are holding the **same** number of bugs.

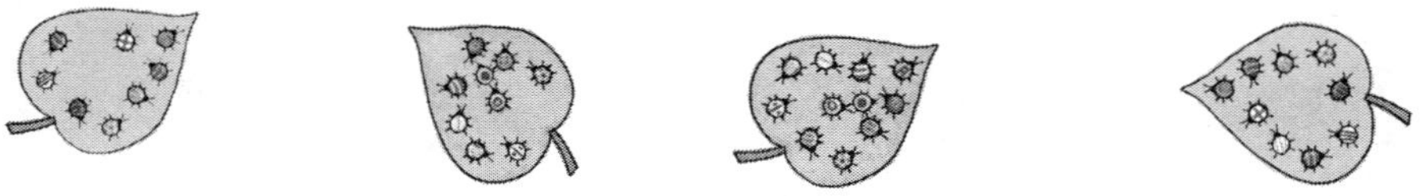

5
1 mark

6 Put the cards in order, **smallest** first.

13 17 9 11   ☐ , ☐ , ☐ , ☐

6
1 mark

7 Circle the **4th** and the **12th** carrots.

7
2 marks

8 Write the missing numbers on the number line.

8 9 10 ☐ 12 ☐ ☐ ☐ 16 ☐ ☐ ☐

8
1 mark

● identify and represent numbers using objects and pictorial
representations including the number line, and use the
language of: equal to, more than, less than (fewer),
most, least

Total: ☐ out of 10   Mastery: NYA   A   A&E

© HarperCollinsPublishers Ltd. 2014

Name: _____   Date: _____

Number and place value

1 Listen carefully. 🔊👤

1	2	3	4	5	6	7	8	9	10

11	12	13	14	15	16	17	18	19	20

1

3 marks

2 Listen carefully. 🔊👤

2

3 marks

3 Draw lines to match the numeral with the word for that number.

four	eighteen	eleven	seven

18	4	7	11

3

4 marks

● read and write numbers from 1 to 20 in numerals and words

Total: ⬜ out of 10   Mastery: NYA | A | A&E

Name: _____   **Date:** _____

Addition and subtraction

1 Write an addition number sentence to show the total number of biscuits on each tray.

a)    ☐ + ☐ = ☐

b) 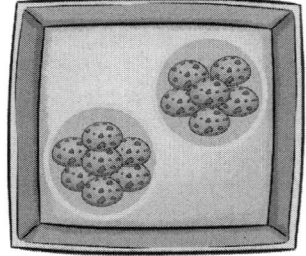   ☐ + ☐ = ☐

2 Write a subtraction number sentence to show the number of birds left on each tree.

a)     ☐ − ☐ = ☐

b)     ☐ − ☐ = ☐

3 a) 5 + 2 = ☐   b) 8 + 5 = ☐

c) 10 − 3 = ☐   d) 13 − 4 = ☐

e) 7 + 4 = ☐   f) 9 − 6 = ☐

● read, write and interpret mathematical statements involving addition (+), subtraction (−) and equals (=) signs

Total: ☐ out of 10   Mastery: NYA | A | A&E

Name: _____   Date: _____

Addition and subtraction

1 a) 3 + 2 = ☐   b) 2 + 1 = ☐

c) 1 + 3 = ☐   d) 5 + 0 = ☐

1 4 marks

2 a) 4 + 3 = ☐   b) 7 + 2 = ☐

c) 6 + 1 = ☐   d) 5 + 4 = ☐

2 4 marks

3 a) 6 + 7 = ☐   b) 7 + 9 = ☐

c) 8 + 4 = ☐   d) 6 + 6 = ☐

e) 9 + 5 = ☐   f) 8 + 7 = ☐

3 6 marks

4 a) 5 – 2 = ☐   b) 3 – 0 = ☐

c) 4 – 3 = ☐   d) 2 – 1 = ☐

4 4 marks

5 a) 8 – 6 = ☐   b) 7 – 5 = ☐

c) 10 – 4 = ☐   d) 9 – 3 = ☐

5 4 marks

6 a) 15 – 6 = ☐   b) 13 – 7 = ☐

c) 19 – 8 = ☐   d) 17 – 9 = ☐

e) 18 – 5 = ☐   f) 14 – 4 = ☐

6 6 marks

7 Write an addition and a subtraction number sentence using these 3 numbers.

☐ + ☐ = ☐   ☐ – ☐ = ☐

7 2 marks

● represent and use number bonds and related subtraction facts within 20

Total: ☐ out of 30   Mastery: NYA | A | A&E

Name: _____   Date: _____

Addition and subtraction

1 a) 12 + 6 = ☐   b) 17 + 2 = ☐

c) 10 + 0 = ☐   d) 3 + 15 = ☐

e) 13 + 4 = ☐   f) 8 + 11 = ☐

g) 1 + 18 = ☐   h) 4 + 16 = ☐

i) 14 + 5 = ☐   j) 0 + 20 = ☐

1
10 marks

2 a) 19 − 8 = ☐   b) 11 − 10 = ☐

c) 13 − 13 = ☐   d) 15 − 7 = ☐

e) 18 − 12 = ☐   f) 12 − 0 = ☐

g) 16 − 9 = ☐   h) 20 − 11 = ☐

i) 14 − 6 = ☐   j) 17 − 5 = ☐

2
10 marks

● add and subtract one-digit and two-digit numbers to 20, including zero

Total: ☐ out of 20   Mastery: NYA | A | A&E

Name: _____   Date: _____

Addition and subtraction

1   **a)** There are 4 flowers in one vase and 8 flowers in the other vase.

How many flowers altogether?

☐ ◯ ☐ ◯ ☐

b) There are 10 sweets in a jar. If Lucy eats 3 of them, how many sweets will be left in the jar?

☐ ◯ ☐ ◯ ☐

c) Jake bought a bag of crisps. What was his change from 20p?

☐ p ◯ ☐ p ◯ ☐ p

d) Clint bought a drink and an ice cream. How much did he spend?

☐ p ◯ ☐ p ◯ ☐ p

1
8 marks

2   **a)** 7 + ☐ = 12

b) ☐ + 6 = 15

c) ☐ − 8 = 2

d) 14 − ☐ = 7

e) 18 = ☐ + 10

f) 6 = ☐ − 5

g) 3 = 11 − ☐

h) 16 = 8 + ☐

i) ☐ + 9 = 20

j) 15 − ☐ = 6

k) ☐ − 6 = 1

l) 13 + ☐ = 13

2
12 marks

● solve one-step problems that involve addition and subtraction, using concrete objects and pictorial representations, and missing number problems such as 7 = ☐ − 9

Total: ☐ out of 20   Mastery: | NYA | A | A&E |

Name: _____ Date: _____

Multiplication and division

1 **a)** 3 lots of 5 is [ ] . **b)** 4 lots of 10 is [ ] . **c)** 7 lots of 2 is [ ] . **1**
3 marks

2 **a)** 6 crayons shared between 2 is [ ] crayons each.

b) 8 cookies shared between 4 is [ ] cookies each.

c) 15 sweets shared between 5 is [ ] sweets each.

2
3 marks

3 **a)** There are 10 pencils in each cup. How many pencils altogether?

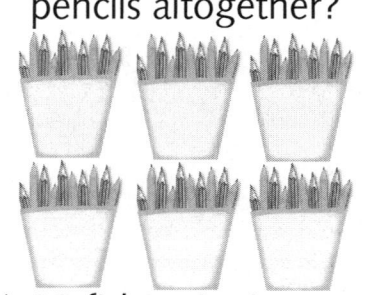 [ ]

b) 3 children share 12 strawberries equally. How many strawberries does each child get?

 [ ]

c) 20 fish swim in groups of 5. How many groups of fish?

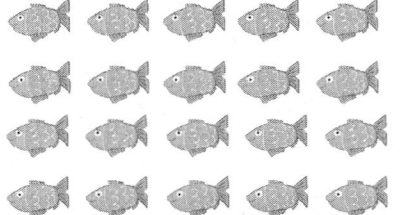 [ ]

d) How much money is in the purse?

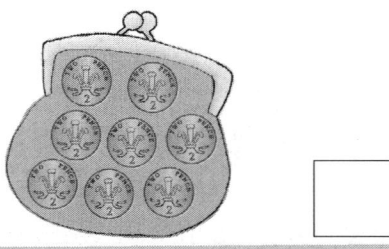 [ ]

3
4 marks

● solve one-step problems involving multiplication and division, by calculating the answer using concrete objects, pictorial representations and arrays with the support of the teacher

Total: [ ] out of 10   Mastery: NYA | A | A&E

Name: _____   Date: _____

Fractions

You will need:
• a coloured pencil

1 Shade half of each shape.

a)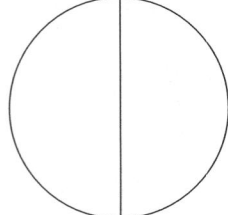

b)

1
2 marks

2 Circle the shapes that show one half shaded grey.

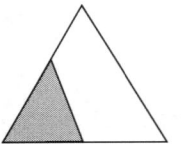 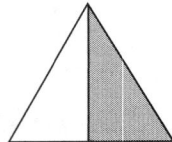 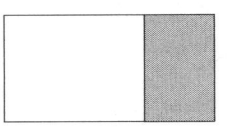 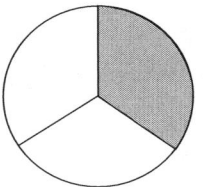 

2
2 marks

3 Circle half of the eggs.

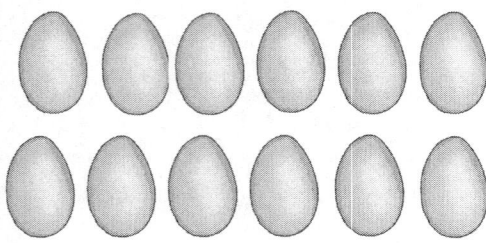

4 Circle half of the apples.

3
1 mark

4
1 mark

5 Half of 10 is ☐.

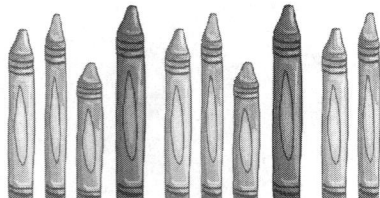

6 Half of 6 is ☐.

5
1 mark

6
1 mark

7 Divide the cake in half.
Colour one half.

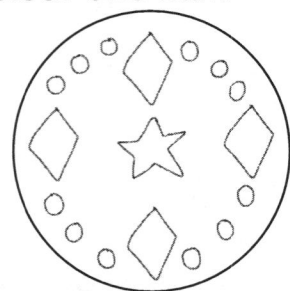

8 Divide the cake in half.
Colour one half.

7
1 mark

8
1 mark

● recognise, find and name one half as one of two equal parts of an object, shape or quantity

Total: ☐ out of 10   Mastery: NYA | A | A&E

© HarperCollinsPublishers Ltd. 2014

Name: _____ Date: _____

Fractions

You will need:
• coloured pencil

1 Shade one quarter of each shape.

a) 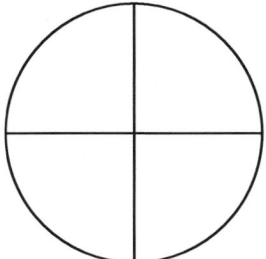   b)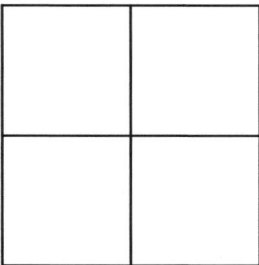

1
2 marks

2 Circle the shapes that show one quarter shaded grey.

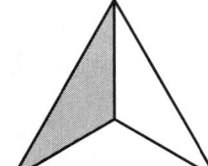 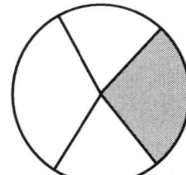 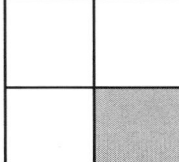  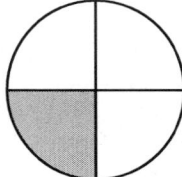

2
2 marks

3 Circle one quarter of the brushes.

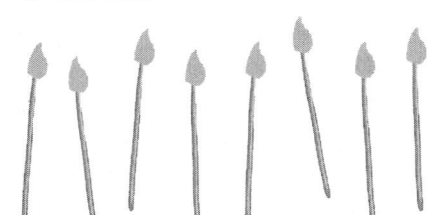

3
1 mark

4 Circle one quarter of the cherries.

4
1 mark

5 One quarter of 20 is ☐.

5
1 mark

6 One quarter of 12 is ☐.

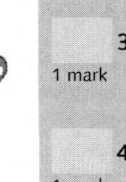 

6
1 mark

7 Divide the cake into quarters. Colour one quarter.

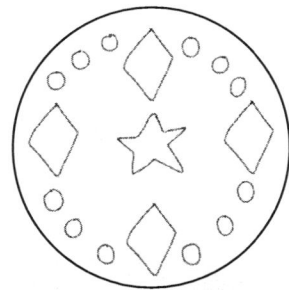

7
1 mark

8 Divide the cake into quarters. Colour one quarter.

8
1 mark

● recognise, find and name one quarter as one of four equal parts of an object, shape or quantity

Total: ☐ out of 10   Mastery: NYA | A | A&E

Name: _____ Date: _____

Measurement

1 Circle the **longer** ribbon.

2 Circle the **taller** child.

3 Circle the **lighter** animal.

4 Circle the **heavier** object.

5 Circle the jug that holds **more**.

6 Circle the glass that has **less** water in it.

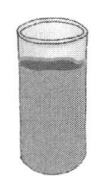 

7 Circle the animal that moves **faster**.

8 Circle the object that moves **slower**.

9 Draw something **heavier** than your shoe.

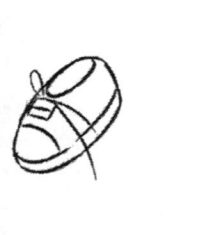

10 Draw something you did **earlier today**.

1
1 mark

2
1 mark

3
1 mark

4
1 mark

5
1 mark

6
1 mark

7
1 mark

8
1 mark

9
1 mark

10
1 mark

● compare, describe and solve practical problems for:
– lengths and heights
– mass/weight
– capacity and volume
– time

Total: _____ out of 10   Mastery: NYA | A | A&E

Name: _____ Date: _____

Measurement

1 Circle the longest worm.

1
1 mark

2 Use a ruler to measure the length of each ribbon

a) ☐ centimetres

b) ☐ centimetres

2
2 marks

3 Circle the **lighter** object.

4 What is the weight of the fruit?

☐ kg

3
1 mark

4
1 mark

5 Circle the container that is **half full.**

6 Circle the two objects that hold **less** than 1 litre.

5
1 mark

6
2 marks

7 What is the time?

☐

8 Circle the **shortest** amount of time.

hour   second

minute   day

7
1 mark

8
1 mark

● measure and begin to record the following:
  – lengths and heights
  – mass/weight
  – capacity and volume
  – time (hours, minutes, seconds)

Total: ☐ out of 10   Mastery: NYA | A | A&E

Name: _____   Date: _____

Measurement

1 Draw lines to match pairs of purses with the same value.

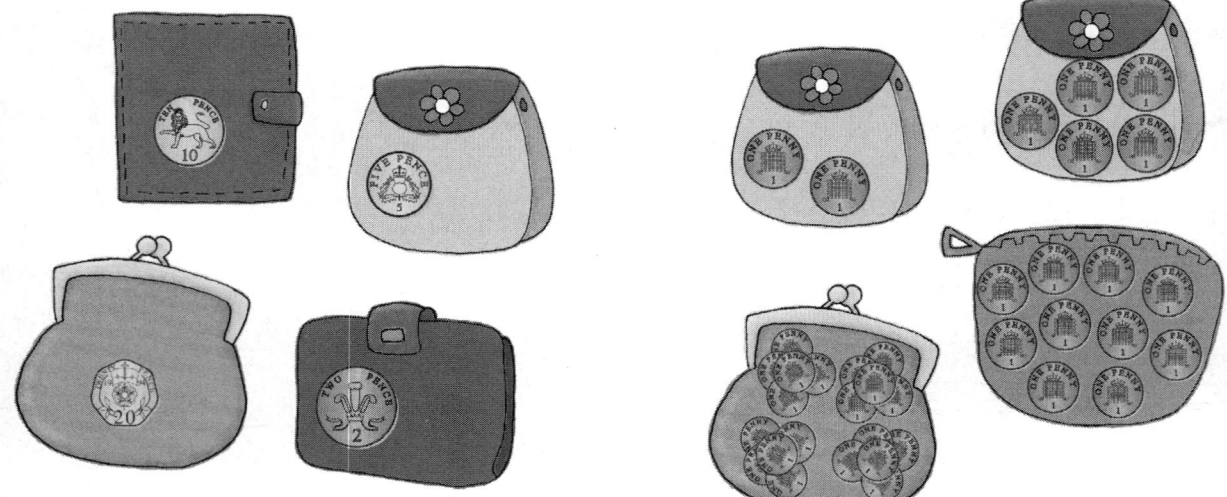

1

4 marks

2 Draw lines to match pairs of purses with the same value.

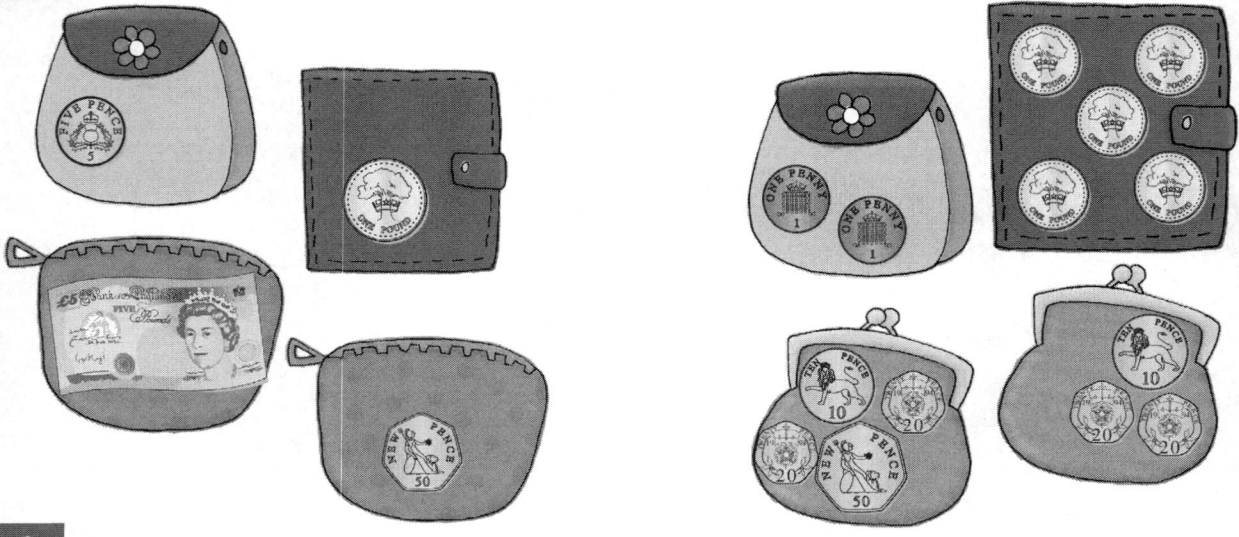

2

4 marks

3 Draw the coins you would use to pay the exact price for each item.

a)

7p

b)

12p

3

2 marks

● recognise and know the value of different denominations of coins and notes   Total: ☐ out of 10   Mastery: NYA | A | A&E

Name: _____   Date: _____

Measurement

1 Draw lines to match the order in which you paint a picture.

| first | second | third | last |

1
4 marks

2 Draw lines to match the order in which you bake a cake.

| first | second | third | last |

2
4 marks

3 Draw lines to match each picture to the correct time of day.

| morning | afternoon | evening |

3
2 marks

● sequence events in chronological order using language
[for example, before and after, next, first, today, yesterday, tomorrow, morning, afternoon and evening]   Total: [____] out of 10   Mastery: NYA   A   A&E

Name: _____   **Date:** _____

Measurement

1 Starting from Monday, draw a line to show the order of the days of the week.

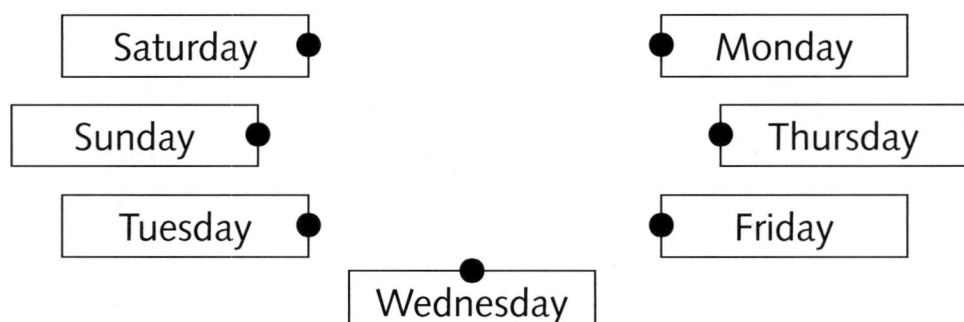

1
1 mark

2 Draw a circle around the 4 months that are **not** in the right order.

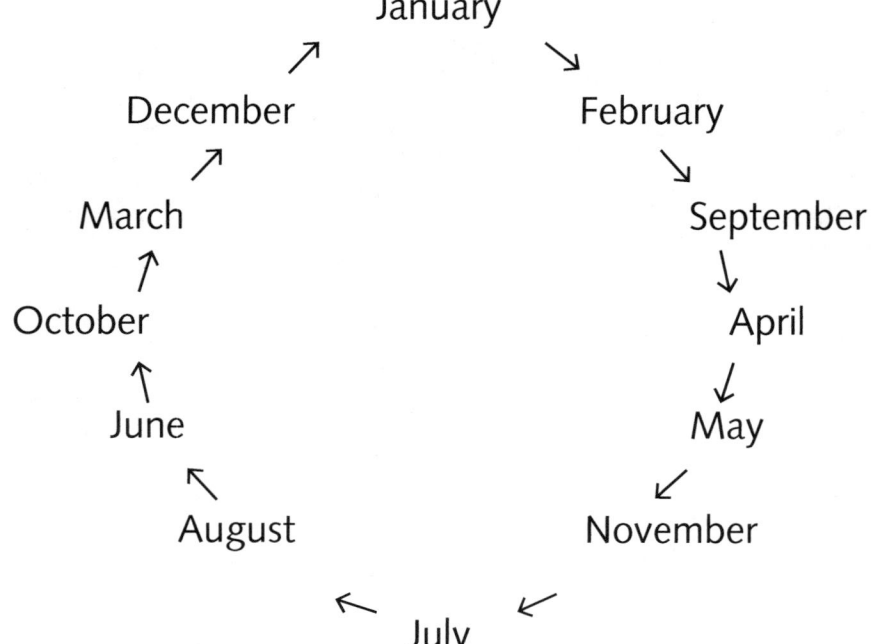

2
4 marks

3 What day of the week is it today? _____

What day of the week was it yesterday? _____

What month of the year is it? _____

What day in the month is it? _____

What year is it? _____

3
5 marks

● recognise and use language relating to dates, including days of the week, weeks, months and years

Total: ☐ out of 10   Mastery: NYA | A | A&E

Name: _____   Date: _____

Measurement

1 Write the times.

a)

b)

c)

d)

e)

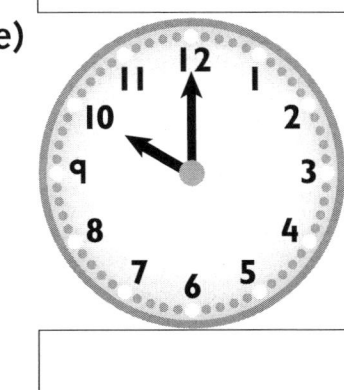

1

5 marks

2 Draw hands on each clock to show the time.

a)

half past 4

b)

2 o'clock

c)

half past 5

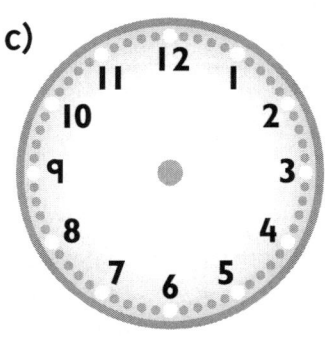

d)

9 o'clock

e)

half past 8

2

5 marks

● tell the time to the hour and half past the hour and draw
the hands on a clock face to show these times

Total: ____ out of 10   Mastery: NYA | A | A&E

Name: _____   Date: _____

Properties of shapes

1   Draw lines to match each shape to its name.

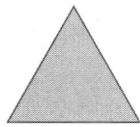         

| circle | square | triangle | rectangle |

   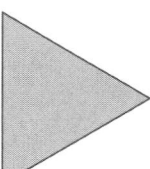      

1
4 marks

2   Draw lines to match each shape to its name.

 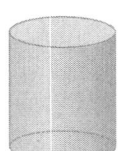 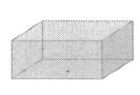  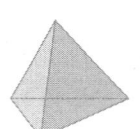 

| cylinder | sphere | cube | pyramid | cone | cuboid |

 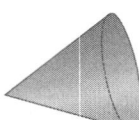  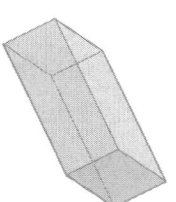 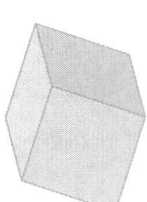 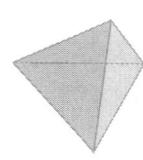

2
6 marks

● recognise and name common 2-D and 3-D shapes,
 including:
 – 2-D shapes
 – 3-D shapes

Total: [ ] out of 10   Mastery: NYA | A | A&E

Name: _____ Date: _____

Position and direction

You will need:
• coloured pencil

1 Listen carefully.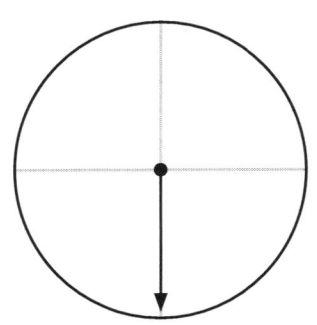

1
7 marks

2 **a)** Draw the arrow after **half** a turn.

b) Draw the arrow after **one quarter** turn to the **right**.

c) Draw the arrow after a **three-quarter** turn to the **right**.

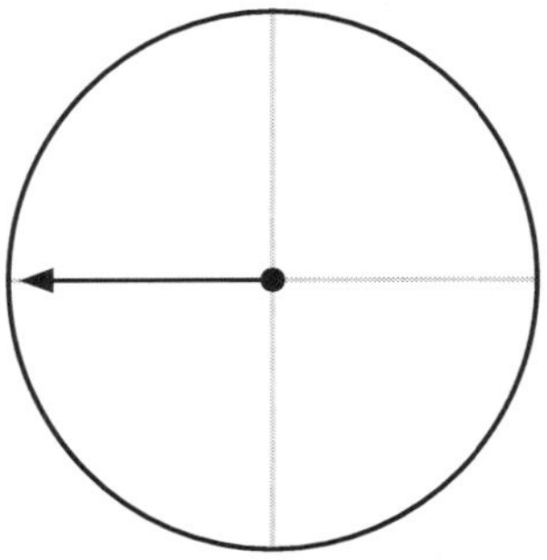

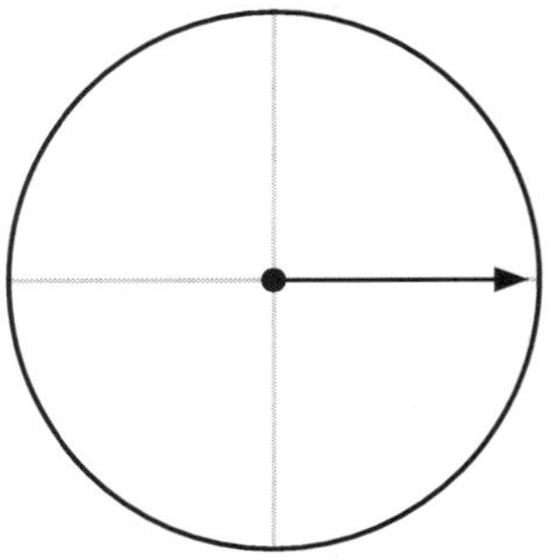

2
3 marks

● describe position, direction and movement, including whole, half, quarter and three-quarter turns

Total: [ ] out of 10   Mastery: NYA A A&E

Year 1 Assessment Exercises – Notes, oral questions, answers and marking commentary

Exercise 1: Number – Number and place value

NOTE Assessment Exercise 1 is designed to be administered orally. The pupil is not expected to read or write the numbers on this sheet. Teachers should read the numbers in each question and ask the pupil to continue the count. The pupil should count forwards or backwards as many times as is considered necessary by the teacher to show the level of mastery achieved. This sheet is intended as a recording sheet of the pupil's responses and should be completed by the teacher.

1 5, 6, 7, 8, 9, 10

2 5, 4, 3, 2, 1, 0

3 6, 7, 8, 9, 10, 11, 12

4 21, 22, 23, 24, 25, 26, 27

5 15, 14, 13, 12, 11, 10, 9

6 58, 59, 60, 61, 62, 63, 64

7 41, 40, 39, 38, 37, 36, 35

8 90, 91, 92, 93, 94, 95, 96

9 72, 71, 70, 69, 68, 67, 66

10 98, 99, 100, 101, 102, 103, 104

Exercise 2: Number – Number and place value

1 10, 12, 14, 16

2 50, 60, 70, 80

3 25, 30, 35, 40

4 50, 60, 80, 90

5 60, 65, 75, 80

6 26, 30, 32, 36

7 18

8 16

9 60

10 25

Exercise 3: Number – Number and place value

1 a) 6 b) 12 c) 20
   d) 17 e) 28

2 a) 11 b) 14 c) 6
   d) 9 e) 22

Exercise 4: Number – Number and place value

1 12 gloves circled

2 Tray on right circled

3 Necklace on left circled

4 a) 7 circled
   b) 15 circled

5 2nd and 4th leaves circled

6 9, 11, 13, 17

7 4th and 12th carrots circled

8 11, 13, 14, 15, 17, 18, 19

Exercise 5: Number – Number and place value

Oral questions

1 *Look at the numbers 1 to 20 at the top of the sheet.*
   a) *Circle the number five.*
   b) *Circle the number 13.*
   c) *Circle the number 16.*

2 a) *Look at the balloon. Write the number 2 on the balloon.*
   b) *Look at the door. Write the number 9 on the door.*
   c) Look at the boat. Write the number 17 on the boat.

1 a) Number 5 circled
   b) Number 13 circled
   c) Number 16 circled

2 a) 2 written on the balloon
   b) 9 written on the door
   c) 17 written on the boat

3 Four – 4
   Eighteen – 18
   Eleven – 11
   Seven – 7

Exercise 6: Number – Addition and subtraction

1 a) 3 + 5 = 8
   b) 7 + 6 = 13

2 a) 7 – 2 = 5
   b) 10 – 6 = 4

3 a) 7 b) 13 c) 7
   d) 9 e) 11 f) 3

Exercise 7: Number – Addition and subtraction

1 These are the addition number facts to 5.
   a) 5 b) 3 c) 4 d) 5

2 These are the addition number facts to 10.
   a) 7 b) 9 c) 7 d) 9

3 These are the addition number facts to 20.
   a) 13 b) 16 c) 12
   d) 12 e) 14 f) 15

4 These are the subtraction number facts to 5.
   a) 3 b) 3 c) 1 d) 1

5 These are the subtraction number facts to 10.
   a) 2 b) 2 c) 6 d) 6

6 These are the subtraction number facts to 20.
   a) 9 b) 6 c) 11
   d) 8 e) 13 f) 10

7 6 + 8 = 14 or 8 + 6 = 14

   14 – 6 = 8 or 14 – 8 = 6

Exercise 8: Number – Addition and subtraction

1 a) 18 b) 19 c) 10 d) 18
   e) 17 f) 19 g) 19 h) 20
   i) 19 j) 20

2 a) 11 b) 1 c) 0 d) 8
   e) 6 f) 12 g) 7 h) 9
   i) 8 j) 12

Exercise 9: Number – Addition and subtraction

1 Award 2 marks per question for the correct answer. If the answer is incorrect, award 1 mark for identifying the correct calculation.
   a) 4 + 8 = 12 b) 10 – 3 = 7
   c) 20p – 15p = 5p d) 8p + 11p = 19p

2 a) 5 b) 9 c) 10 d) 7
   e) 8 f) 11 g) 8 h) 8
   i) 11 j) 9 k) 7 l) 0

Exercise 10: Number – Multiplication and division

1 a) 15 b) 40 c) 14

2 a) 3 b) 2 c) 3

3 a) 60 b) 4 c) 4 d) 16p

Exercise 11: Number – Fractions

1 a) One half shaded
   b) Two quarters shaded

2 2nd and 5th shapes shaded

3 6 eggs circled

4 4 apples circled

5 5

6 3

7 Line dividing the cake in half; one half coloured

8 Line dividing the cake in half; one half coloured

Exercise 12: Number – Fractions

1 a) One quarter shaded
   b) One quarter shaded

2 3rd and 5th shapes shaded

3 2 brushes circled

4 4 cherries circled

5 5

6 3

7 Lines dividing the cake in quarters; one quarter coloured

8 Lines dividing the cake in quarters; one quarter coloured

Exercise 13: Measurement

1 Longer ribbon circled

2 Taller pupil circled

3 Mouse circled

4 Chair circled

5 Large jug circled

6 Glass with less water circled

7 Cheetah circled

8 Bicycle circled

9 Answers will vary

10 Answers will vary

Exercise 14: Measurement

1 Longest worm circled

2 a) 10 cm
  b) 15 cm

3 Egg circled

4 3 kg

5 Glass circled

6 Spoon and glass circled

7 5 o'clock

8 'second' circled

Exercise 15: Measurement

1

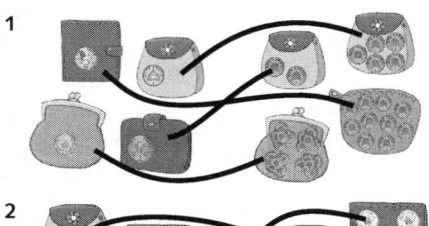

2

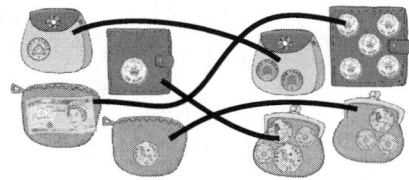

3 a) Answers will vary
  b) Answers will vary

Exercise 16: Measurement

1

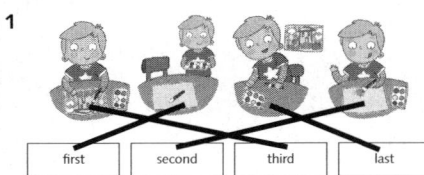

2

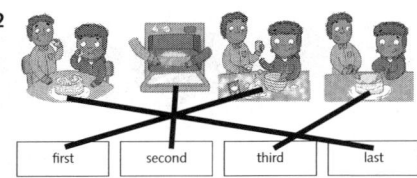

3

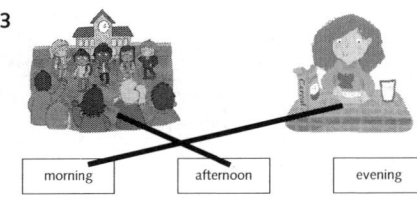

Exercise 17: Measurement

1 Monday – Tuesday – Wednesday – Thursday – Friday – Saturday – Sunday

2 September, November, June and March circled

3 Answers will vary

Exercise 18: Measurement

1 a) 4 o'clock
  b) 7 o'clock
  c) Half past 2
  d) Half past 11
  e) 10 o'clock

2 a)

b)

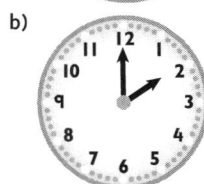

c)

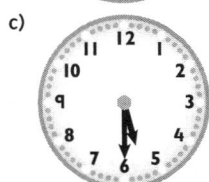

d)

e)

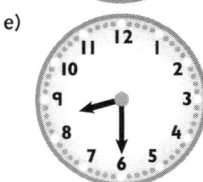

Exercise 19: Geometry – Properties of shapes

1 Correct shapes matched to their names

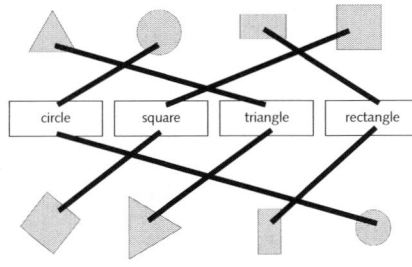

2 Correct shapes matched to their names

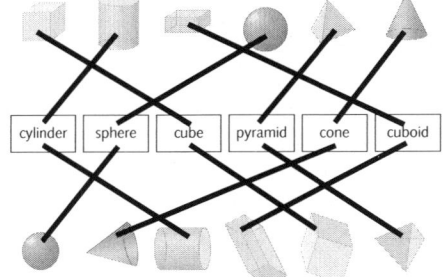

Exercise 20: Geometry – Position and direction

Oral questions

1 Look at the picture of the park.
  a) Draw a circle around what you can see **below** the kite.
  b) Draw a cross through what you can see **behind** the tree.
  c) Tick what you can see **underneath** the ice cream cart.
  d) Draw a circle around what you can see **between** the two children eating ice-creams.
  e) Colour what you can see **in** the tree.
  f) Draw a cross through what you can see **above** the bench.
  g) Colour what you can see to the **left** of the bench.

1 a) People having a picnic circled
  b) Cross drawn through dog
  c) Rucksack ticked
  d) Lady on bench circled
  e) Cat in tree coloured
  f) Cross drawn through bird above the bench
  g) Rubbish bin coloured

2 a)

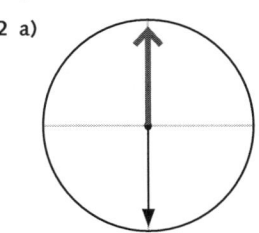

b)

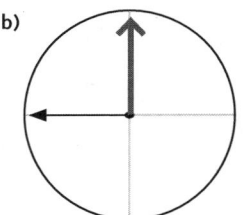

c)

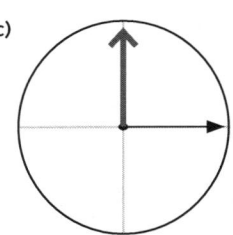

1 Write the missing numbers.

a) 0, 1, 2, 3, 4, ☐ , ☐

b) 14, 15, ☐ , ☐ , 18, 19, 20

 1
2 marks

2 Write the number that is **1 more**.

a) 9 ☐   b) 12 ☐

 2
2 marks

3 Write the number that is **1 less**.

a) 18 ☐   b) 11 ☐

 3
2 marks

4   a) How many  ? ☐   b) How many  ? ☐

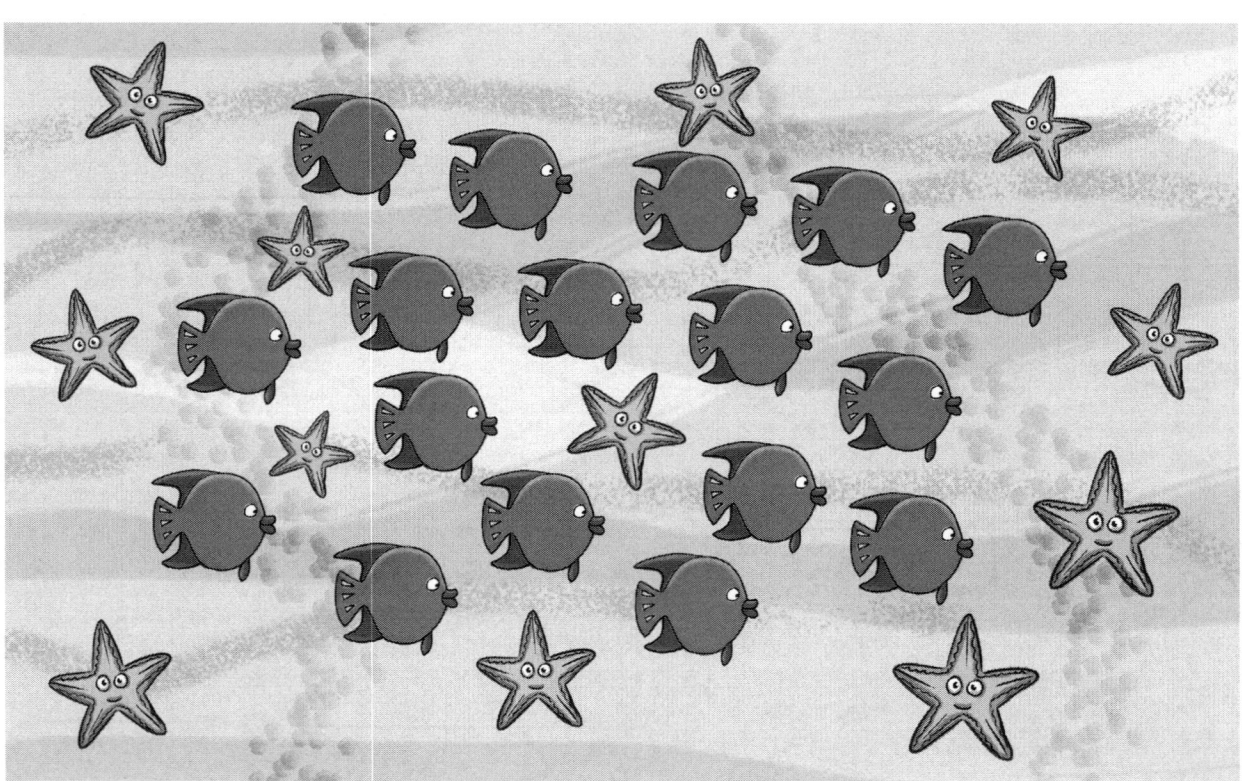

4
2 marks

5 Circle the **7th** and the **12th** shells.

5
2 marks

Name: _____ Date: _____

1 How many shells does each child have?
Write the addition number sentence and the answer.

a)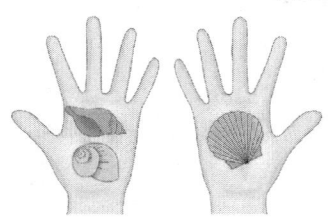

b)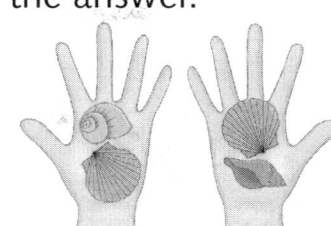

☐ + ☐ = ☐   ☐ + ☐ = ☐

1
2 marks

2 Use the number track to work out the answer.

a)

① ② ③ ④ ⑤

3 + 2 = ☐

b)

① ② ③ ④ ⑤

1 + 3 = ☐

2
2 marks

3 Take away 2 fish from each rock pool.
Write the subtraction number sentence and the answer.

a)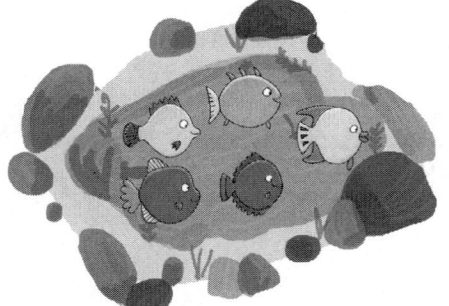

b)

☐ – ☐ = ☐   ☐ – ☐ = ☐

3
2 marks

4 Use the number track to work out the answer.

a)

① ② ③ ④ ⑤

3 – 1 = ☐

b)

① ② ③ ④ ⑤

4 – 3 = ☐

4
2 marks

5 a) 5 – 4 = ☐   b) 3 + 0 = ☐

5
2 marks

Year 1 | Unit 1 | Week 2: Addition and subtraction   Total: ☐ out of 10   Mastery: NYA   A   A&E

1 Look at the shapes above.
a) **Colour** all the **circles**.
b) Draw a **tick (✓)** inside each **square**.
c) Draw a (ring) around each **rectangle**.
d) Draw a **cross (✗)** inside each **triangle**.

1
4 marks

2 How many sides does each shape have?

a) square [ ]   b) triangle [ ]   c) circle [ ]

2
3 marks

3 How many corners does each shape have?

a) rectangle [ ]   b) circle [ ]   c) triangle [ ]

3
3 marks

Year 1 | Unit 1 | Week 3: Properties of shapes   Total: [ ] out of 10 Mastery: NYA A A&E

Name: _____   Date: _____

1　a) 3 + 5 = ☐　　　　b) 2 + 4 = ☐

　　c) 4 + 3 = ☐　　　　d) 6 + 3 = ☐

1 4 marks

2　a) 8 − 2 = ☐　　　　b) 10 − 9 = ☐

　　c) 6 − 4 = ☐　　　　d) 9 − 3 = ☐

2 4 marks

3　Double each of these numbers.

　　a) 2 ☐　　　　b) 5 ☐　　　　c) 3 ☐

3 3 marks

4　Work out the answer to each fact.

Then draw a line from each addition fact to its matching subtraction fact.

3 + 2 = ☐　　　　7 − 2 = ☐

6 + 4 = ☐　　　　5 − 3 = ☐

2 + 5 = ☐　　　　10 − 6 = ☐

4 9 marks

　　Total: ☐ out of 20　Mastery: NYA　A　A&E

1 Work out the answer to each addition fact.

Then draw a line between each pair of matching addition facts.

5 + 4 = ☐   3 + 7 = ☐

7 + 3 = ☐   2 + 6 = ☐

6 + 2 = ☐   4 + 5 = ☐

9 marks

2 Use the number track to work out the answer.

a) 8 − 3 = ☐ ① ② ③ ④ ⑤ ⑥ ⑦ ⑧ ⑨ ⑩

b) 10 − 7 = ☐ ① ② ③ ④ ⑤ ⑥ ⑦ ⑧ ⑨ ⑩

2 marks

3 a) 3 + ☐ = 7   b) 6 − ☐ = 2   c) 9 − ☐ = 4

d) ☐ + 3 = 8   e) ☐ − 4 = 6

5 marks

4 a) Tim is holding 6 pencils. He drops 2 pencils. How many pencils is Tim left holding?

b) Ellie is holding 3 pencils in one hand and 5 pencils in her other hand. How many pencils is Ellie holding altogether?

4 marks

Name: _____ Date: _____

1 Circle the longest ribbon.

You will need:
• ruler

1 1 mark

2 Circle the shortest rope.

2 1 mark

3 Circle the tallest tree.

4 Circle the shortest flagpole.

3 1 mark

4 1 mark

5 Use a ruler to measure each object.

a) ☐ centimetres

b) ☐ centimetres

c) ☐ centimetres

5 3 marks

6 a) Use a ruler to draw a line of 10 cm.

b) Use the ruler to draw a line of 13 cm.

6 2 marks

7 Use a ruler to draw a line shorter than this line.

7 1 mark

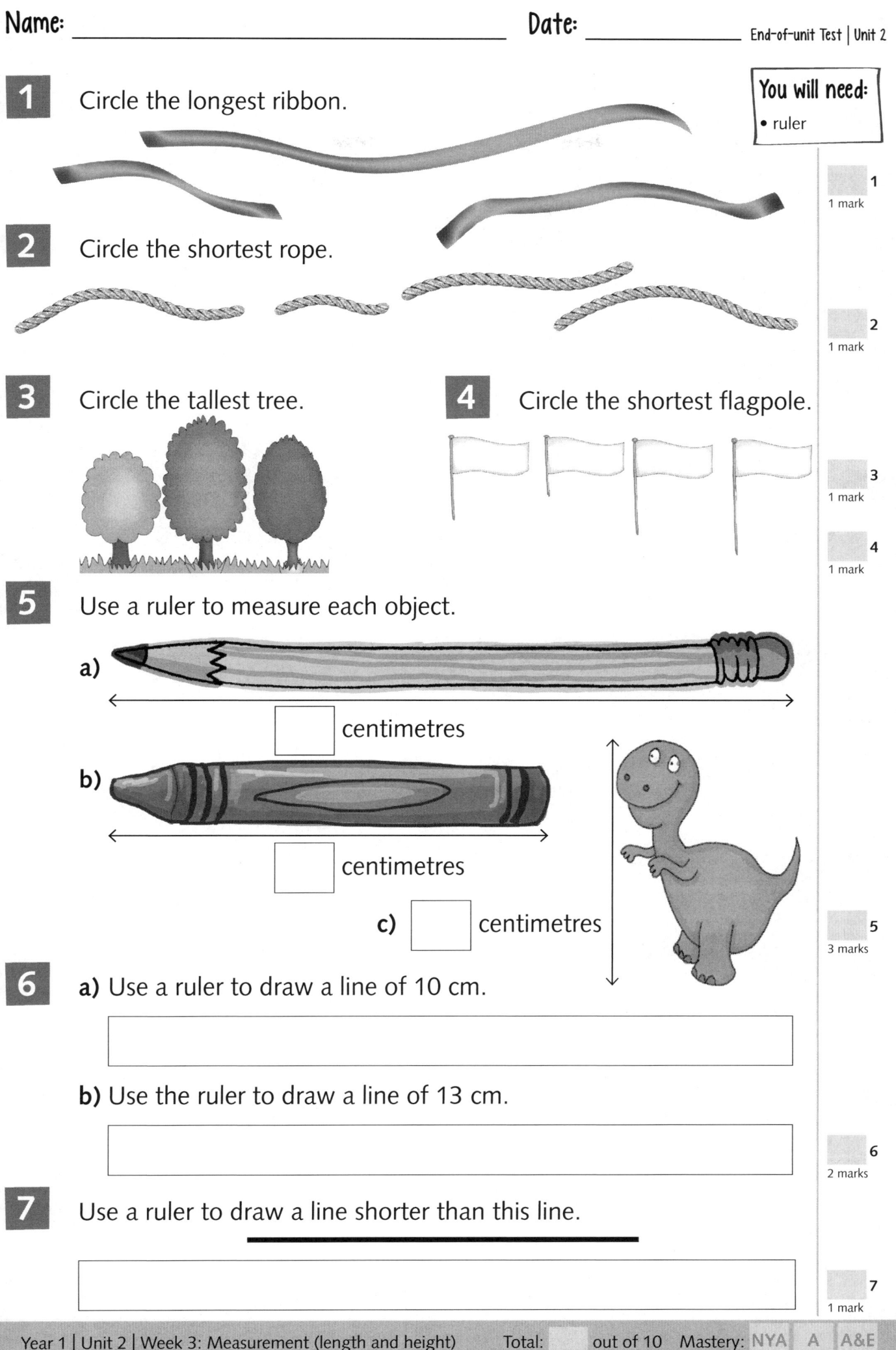

Continue each number pattern.

1 0 2 4 6 ☐ ☐ 12

	1
	1 mark

2 0 5 10 15 ☐ ☐ 30

	2
	1 mark

3 0 10 20 30 ☐ ☐ 60

	3
	1 mark

4 20 25 ☐ 35 40 ☐ 50

	4
	1 mark

5 8 10 ☐ 14 ☐ 18 20

	5
	1 mark

6 40 50 60 ☐ 80 ☐ 100

	6
	1 mark

7 20 18 16 ☐ 12 10 ☐

	7
	1 mark

8 30 25 ☐ 15 ☐ 5 0

	8
	1 mark

9 70 60 ☐ 40 30 ☐ 10

	9
	1 mark

10 18 20 ☐ 24 26 ☐ 30

	10
	1 mark

Name: _____   Date: _____   End-of-unit Test | Unit 3

1 **a)** How many pots? ☐

b) How many flowers in a pot? ☐

c) How many flowers altogether? ☐

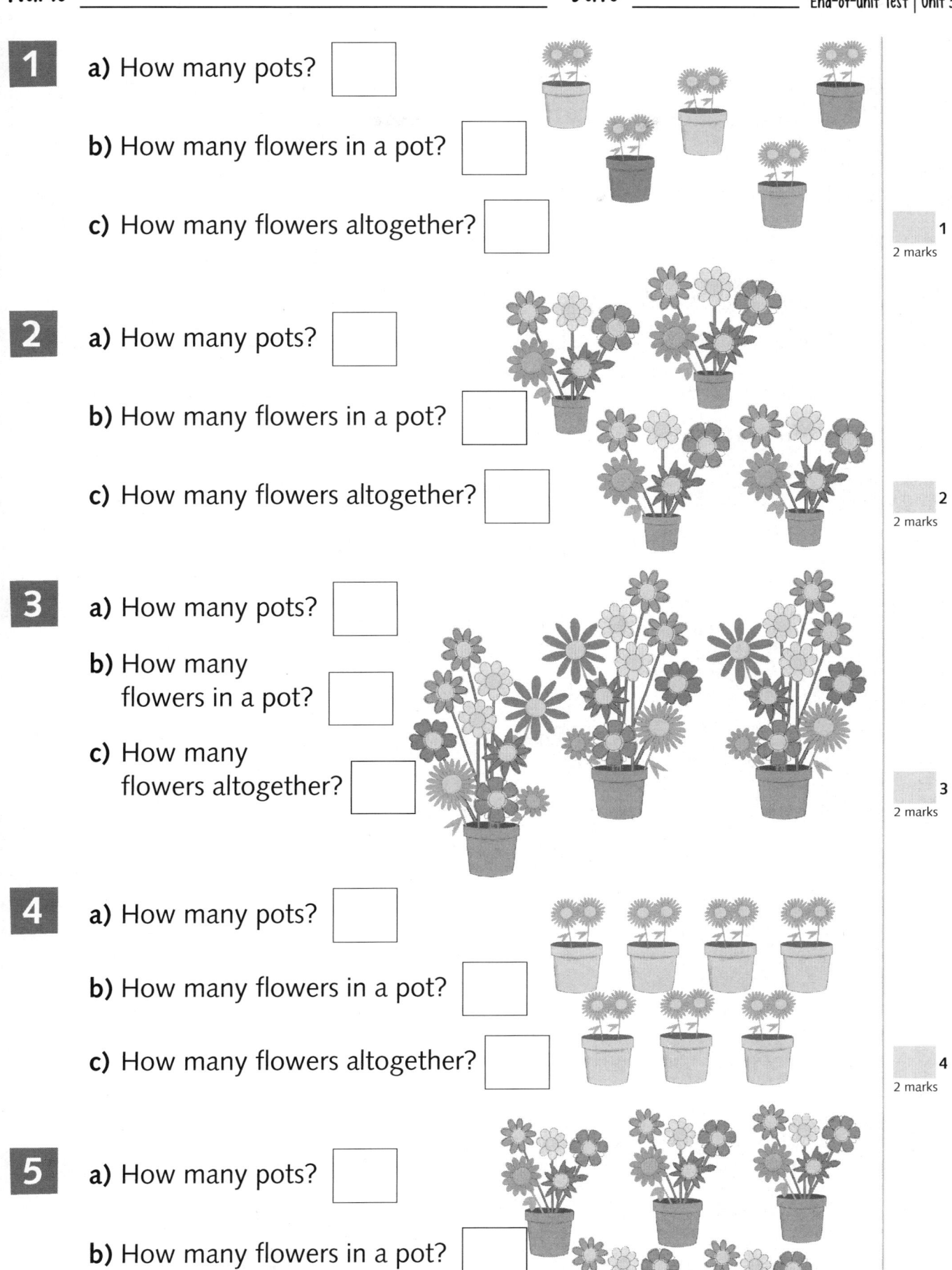

1
2 marks

2 **a)** How many pots? ☐

b) How many flowers in a pot? ☐

c) How many flowers altogether? ☐

2
2 marks

3 **a)** How many pots? ☐

b) How many flowers in a pot? ☐

c) How many flowers altogether? ☐

3
2 marks

4 **a)** How many pots? ☐

b) How many flowers in a pot? ☐

c) How many flowers altogether? ☐

4
2 marks

5 **a)** How many pots? ☐

b) How many flowers in a pot? ☐

c) How many flowers altogether? ☐

5
2 marks

Year 1 | Unit 3 | Week 2: Multiplication and division   Total: ☐ out of 10   Mastery: NYA   A   A&E

© HarperCollins© HarperCollins*Publishers* Ltd. 2014

You will need:
• coloured pencil

1 Circle the cup to the **right** of the bowl.

1
1 mark

2 Circle the glass to the **left** of the jug.

2
1 mark

3 a) Draw a below the FLOUR .

b) Draw a TEA above the RICE .

c) Draw a between the FLOUR and the RICE .

3
3 marks

4 a) Draw the arrow after **half** a turn.

b) Draw the arrow after **one quarter** turn to the right.

c) Draw the arrow after a **three-quarter** turn to the right.

4
3 marks

5 a) The child sitting on the rug makes **one quarter turn** to the **left**. Colour what she is now facing.

b) The child sitting on the rug makes **half a turn**. Circle what she is now facing.

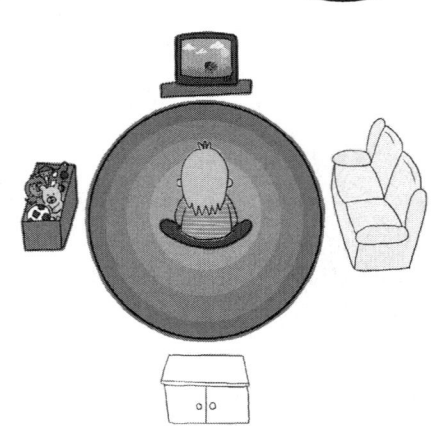

5
2 marks

1

a) 7 + 4 = ☐

b) 3 + 9 = ☐

c) 8 + 5 = ☐

d) 6 + 7 = ☐

e) 7 + 8 = ☐

f) 5 + 9 = ☐

1
6 marks

2

a) 13 − 6 = ☐

b) 14 − 5 = ☐

c) 12 − 9 = ☐

d) 15 − 7 = ☐

e) 14 − 3 = ☐

f) 11 − 8 = ☐

2
6 marks

3

a) 12 − ☐ = 7

b) 6 + ☐ = 14

c) 9 + ☐ = 15

d) 13 − ☐ = 5

3
4 marks

4

a) Ollie has 5 marbles. Lee has 7 marbles. How many marbles do they have altogether?

b) Larry has 13 marbles. He gives 4 to Mel. How many marbles does Larry have left?

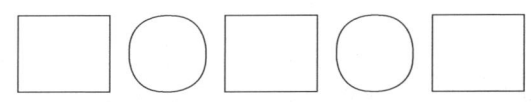

4
4 marks

Total: ☐ out of 20   Mastery: NYA A A&E

Name: _____ Date: _____

You will need:
• coloured pencil

1 Circle the shapes that show one half shaded.

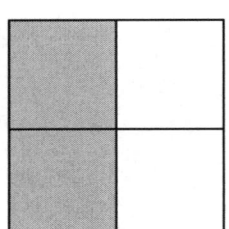 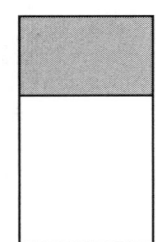 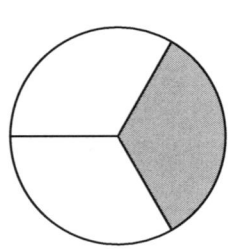 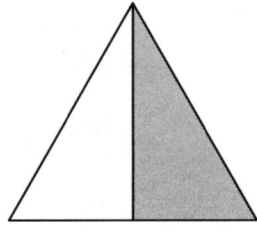

1
2 marks

2 Circle half of the apples.

3 This scarf is 8 cm long. How long is half this scarf? ☐ cm

2
1 mark

3
1 mark

4 Half of 4 is ☐.

5 Half of 12 is ☐.

4
1 mark

5
1 mark

6 Divide the pear in half. Colour one half.

7 Divide the pineapple in half. Colour one half.

6
1 mark

7
1 mark

8 8 orange halves. How many whole oranges? ☐

9 12 orange halves. How many whole oranges? ☐

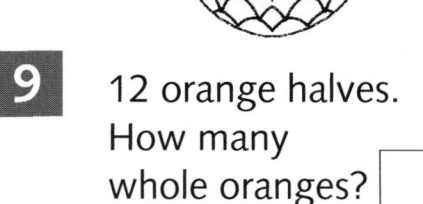

8
1 mark

9
1 mark

Year 1 | Unit 4 | Week 2: Fractions

Total: ☐ out of 10   Mastery: NYA   A   A&E

1 Draw lines to match purses that are holding the same value.

1
4 marks

2 Draw the coins you would use to pay the exact price for each item.

a)  Chocolate 8p

b)  Sweets 11p

2
2 marks

3

 4 p   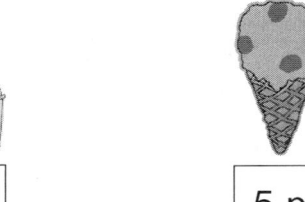 5 p    3 p

a) How much for a  and a  ?   ☐ p

How much change from 10 p?   ☐ p

b) How much for a  and a  ?   ☐ p

How much change from 10 p?   ☐ p

3
4 marks

1 Write each set of numbers in order, smallest to largest.

a) 6, 8, 7, 5   ☐ , ☐ , ☐ , ☐

b) 12, 18, 9, 14   ☐ , ☐ , ☐ , ☐

c) 13, 10, 17, 8   ☐ , ☐ , ☐ , ☐

d) 19, 14, 16, 11   ☐ , ☐ , ☐ , ☐

1
4 marks

2 Circle all the even numbers.

5   8   13   14   16   19   20

2
1 mark

3 Circle all the odd numbers.

3   6   9   10   15   17   18

3
1 mark

4 Continue each pattern.

a) ○ △ ○ △ ○ ☐ ☐ ☐

b) △ ▼ △ ▼ △ ☐ ☐ ☐

c) ● ● ○ ● ● ○ ● ☐ ☐ ☐

d) ■ △ ○ ■ △ ○ ■ ☐ ☐ ☐

4
4 marks

1 What change would you get for buying each chocolate with the coin shown?

a)  6 p ☐ p

b) 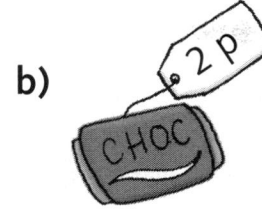 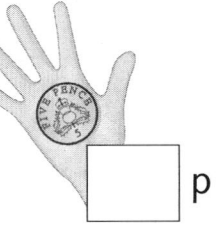 ☐ p

1 2 marks

2  2 p 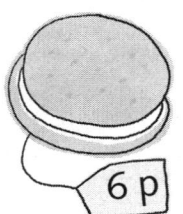 6 p 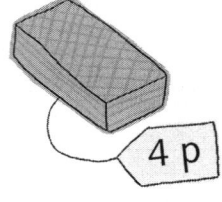 4 p

a) How much for a  and a ⬡ ?

☐ p + ☐ p = ☐ p

b) How much for a ▭ and a ⬭ ?

☐ p + ☐ p = ☐ p

2 2 marks

3 Circle the coins in the purse you would use to pay for the item.

a) 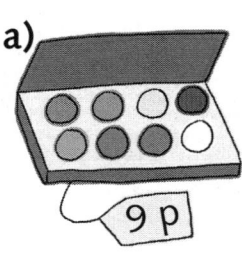 9 p

b)  6 p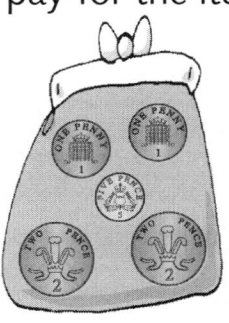

3 2 marks

4 a) Lottie has 12 p. She buys a  10 p

How much does she have left? ☐ p ◯ ☐ p ◯ ☐ p

b) Joe buys a  8 p 6 p

How much does he spend? ☐ p ◯ ☐ p ◯ ☐ p

4 4 marks

1 Draw lines to match each shape to its name.

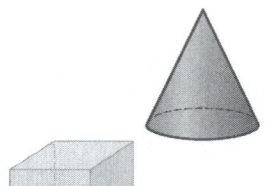

| cube |
| cylinder |
| cone |
| pyramid |
| cuboid |
| sphere |

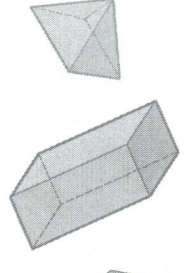

1
6 marks

2 Circle all the cubes.

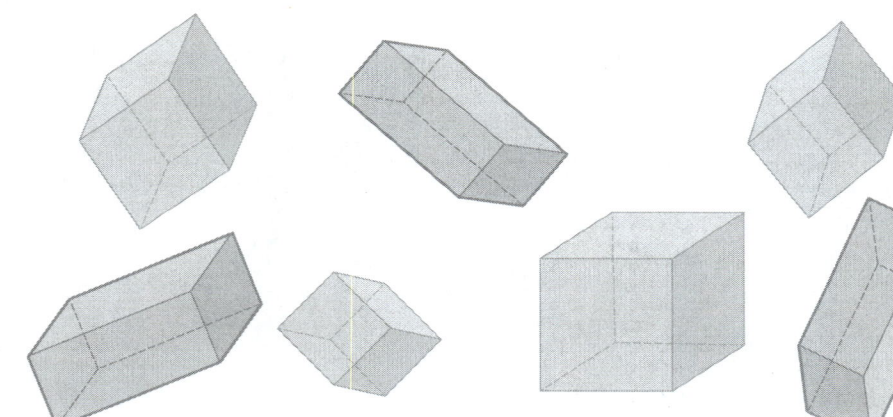
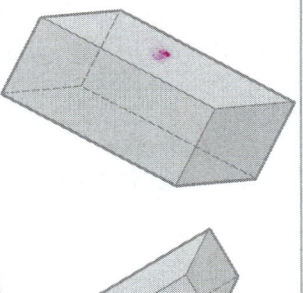

2
2 marks

3 Circle all the 2-D shapes.

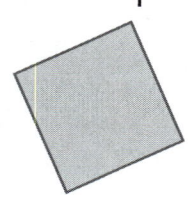
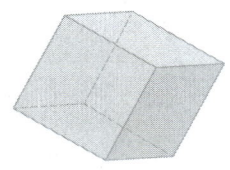

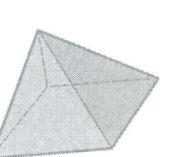
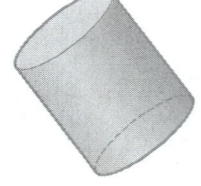
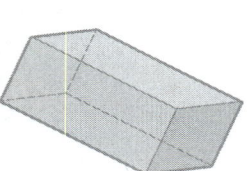

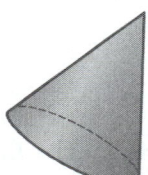

3
2 marks

1 Complete each number pattern.

a) | 5 | 10 | 15 | | | 30 | 35 |

b) | 12 | 14 | | 18 | 20 | 22 | |

c) | 30 | | 50 | 60 | | 80 | 90 |

d) | 28 | 26 | | 22 | 20 | | 16 |

e) | 20 | 25 | | 35 | 40 | 45 | |

f) | 100 | 90 | | 70 | 60 | | 40 |

6 marks

2 How many stars on each rug?

a)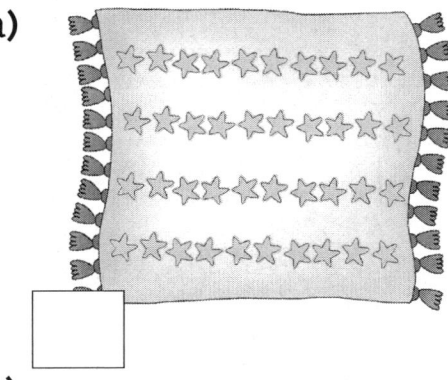

b)

c)

d)

4 marks

1

a) [ ] sets of [ ] make [ ] altogether.

b) [ ] sets of [ ] make [ ] altogether.

c) [ ] sets of [ ] make [ ] altogether.

1
3 marks

2

a) [ ] shared between [ ] is [ ].

b) [ ] shared between [ ] is [ ].

c) [ ] shared between [ ] is [ ].

2
3 marks

3

a) 15 party cakes shared between 5 friends. How many cakes does each friend get? [ ]

b) There are 5 party hats in each bag. How many hats are in 4 bags? [ ]

c) Each bag has 10 balloons. How many balloons are in 3 bags? [ ]

d) 12 children are put into two teams. How many children are in each team? [ ]

3
4 marks

Year 1 | Unit 6 | Week 2: Multiplication and division   Total: [ ] out of 10   Mastery: NYA   A   A&E

1 Circle the **heavier** object.

2 Circle the **lighter** object.

3 Circle the **heaviest** object.

4 Circle the **lightest** object.

5 Circle the **heavier** fruit.

6 Circle the **lighter** fruits.

  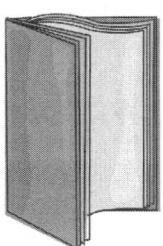

7 What is the weight of each bag of vegetables?

a)

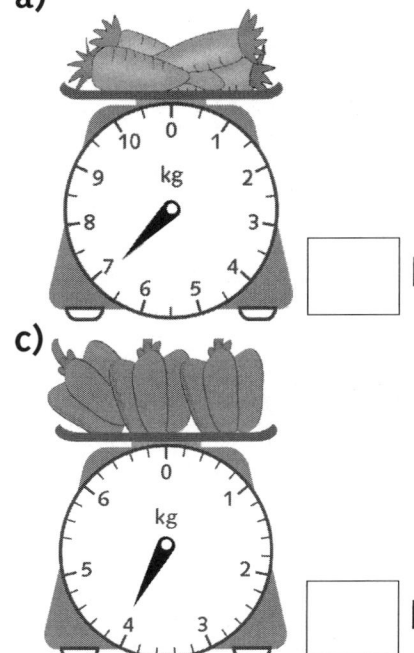 [ ] kilograms

b)

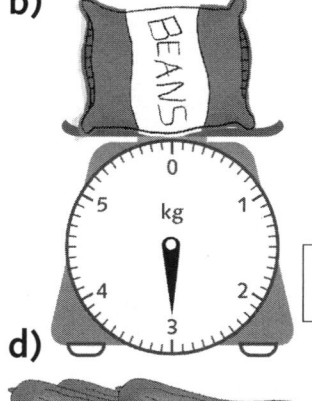 [ ] kilograms

c)

[ ] kilograms

d)

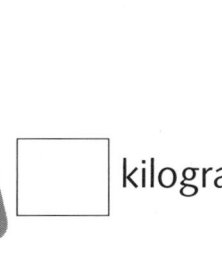 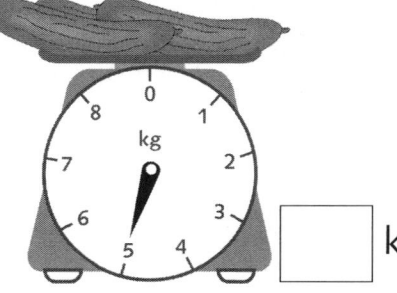 [ ] kilograms

1 — 1 mark
2 — 1 mark
3 — 1 mark
4 — 1 mark
5 — 1 mark
6 — 1 mark
7 — 4 marks

1

a) 3 + ☐ = 10

b) 2 + ☐ = 10

c) 4 + ☐ = 10

d) 5 + ☐ = 10

1
4 marks

2

a) 3 + 4 = ☐

b) 4 + 5 = ☐

c) 2 + 3 = ☐

d) 5 + 6 = ☐

2
4 marks

3 Work out the answer to each fact.

Then draw a line from each addition fact to its matching subtraction fact.

| 6 + 3 = ☐ |

| 8 – 7 = ☐ |

| 2 + 4 = ☐ |

| 10 – 8 = ☐ |

| 7 + 1 = ☐ |

| 6 – 2 = ☐ |

| 8 + 2 = ☐ |

| 9 – 6 = ☐ |

3
12 marks

0 1 2 3 4 5 6 7 8 9 10 11 12 13 14 15

1 Add each pair of numbers. Write the addition fact and the answer.

a)

☐ + ☐ = ☐

b) 6 8

☐ + ☐ = ☐

c) 11 3

☐ + ☐ = ☐

d) 5 10

☐ + ☐ = ☐

1
4 marks

2 Subtract the smaller number from the larger number.
Write the subtraction fact and the answer.

a) 13 8

☐ – ☐ = ☐

b) 12 4

☐ – ☐ = ☐

c) 15 7

☐ – ☐ = ☐

d) 14 5

☐ – ☐ = ☐

2
4 marks

3 a) 7 + ☐ = 13

b) 14 – ☐ = 10

c) 12 + ☐ = 15

d) 11 – ☐ = 5

e) 8 + ☐ = 12

f) 13 – ☐ = 4

4 a) 5 + ☐ = 10

b) 6 + ☐ = 10

c) ☐ + 3 = 10

d) 8 + 2 = ☐

e) 9 + ☐ = 10

f) ☐ + 0 = 10

3
6 marks

4
6 marks

Name: ______________________________ Date: ______________

1 Draw lines to show the answers.

a) The day before Wednesday

b) The day after Friday

Monday

Saturday

Tuesday

1 — 2 marks

2 Draw lines to show the answers.

a) The month before June

b) The month after February.

March

May

August

2 — 2 marks

3 Circle the season that comes after Spring.

winter autumn summer

3 — 1 mark

4 Draw lines to match the order in which you have a meal.

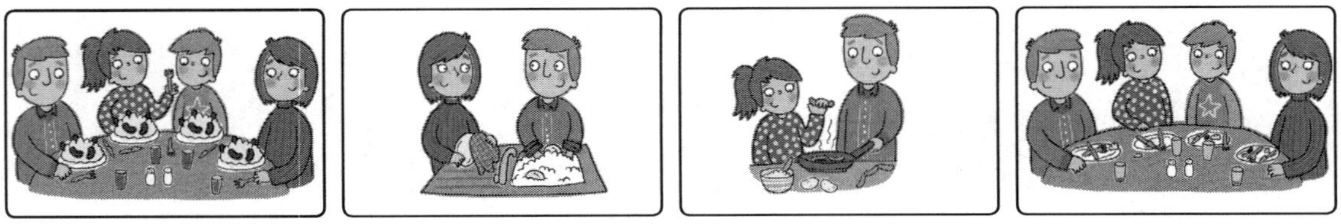

first second third last

4 — 1 mark

5 Write the times.

a)

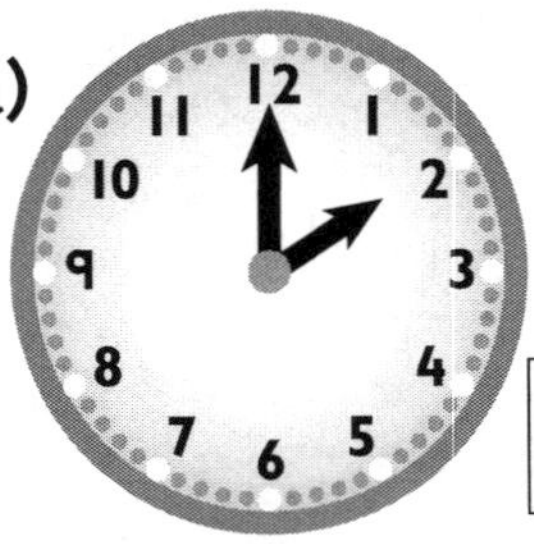

b)

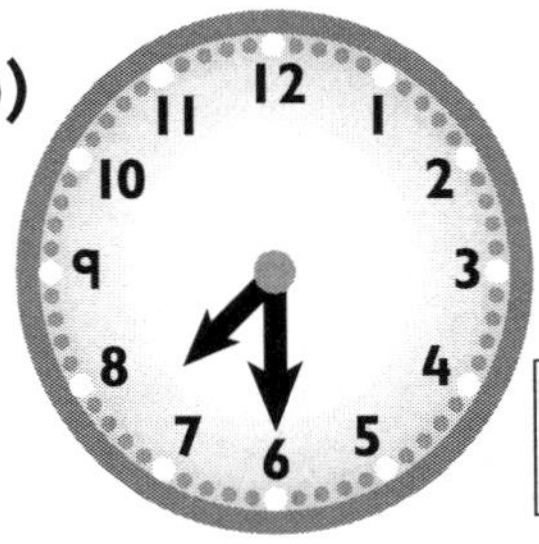

5 — 2 marks

6 Draw hands on each clock to show the time.

a) half past 11

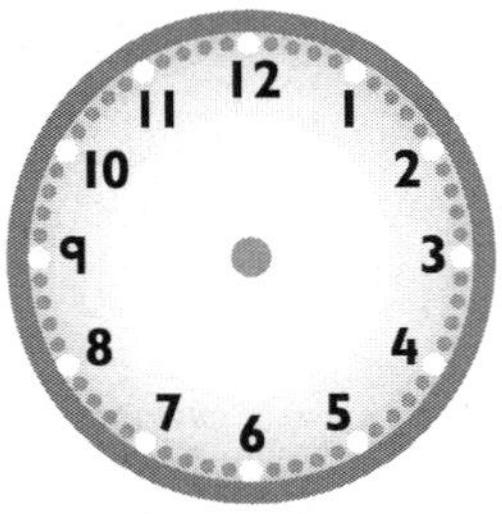

b) 8 o'clock

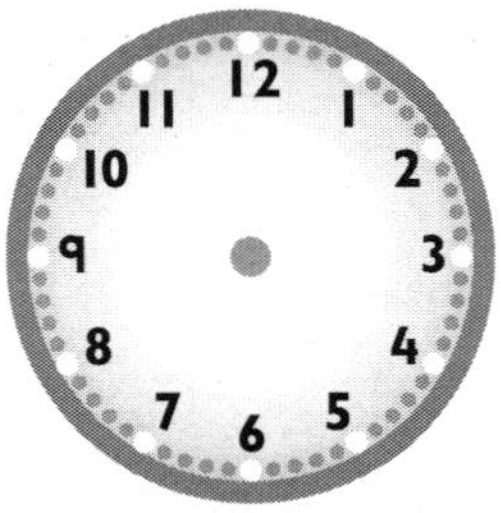

6 — 2 marks

Total: out of 10 Mastery: NYA A A&E

Name: _____ Date: _____

1 Write each numeral as a word.

a) 4 [_____]

b) 7 [_____]

c) 5 [_____]

d) 8 [_____]

1
4 marks

2 Draw lines to match each number.

[14]   [20]   [11]   [17]

[10 + 1]   [10 + 4]   [10 + 7]   [10 + 10]

2
4 marks

3 Write the number that is **1 more**.

a) 15 [ ]   b) 8 [ ]   c) 19 [ ]

3
3 marks

4 Write the number that is **1 less**.

a) 6 [ ]   b) 18 [ ]   c) 11 [ ]

4
3 marks

5 Put the cards in order, smallest first.

     [ ] [ ] [ ] [ ]

5
1 mark

6 a) How many bugs? [ ]   b) How many bugs? [ ]

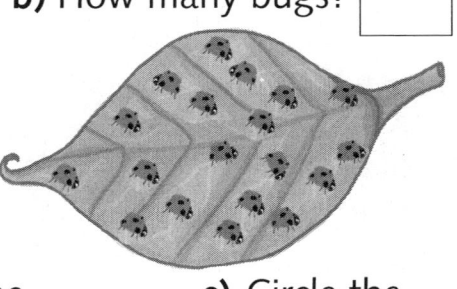

6
2 marks

7 a) Circle the multiples of 2.   b) Circle the multiples of 5.   c) Circle the multiples of 10.

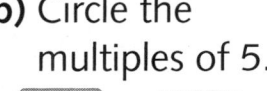 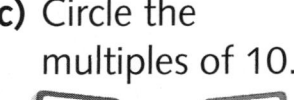

6   9   30   24   8   49

17   18   12   15   20   40

7
3 marks

Year 1 | Unit 8 | Week 1: Number and place value   Total: [ ] out of 20   Mastery: NYA A A&E

© HarperCollins*Publishers* Ltd. 2014

Name: _____ Date: _____

1 Circle the shapes that show one quarter shaded.

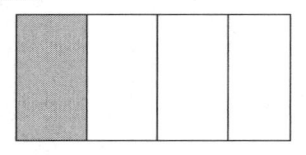 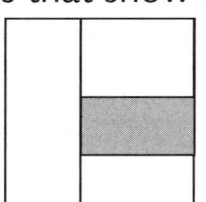 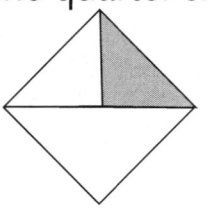 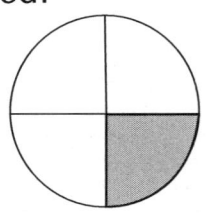

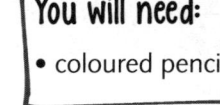 **1** 2 marks

2 Circle one quarter of the buttons.

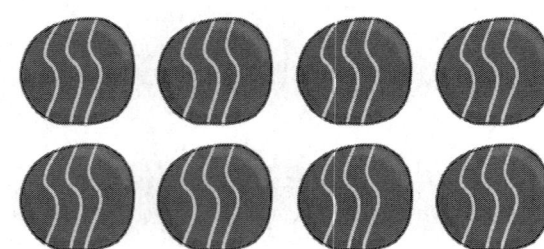

3 Circle one quarter of the buttons.

 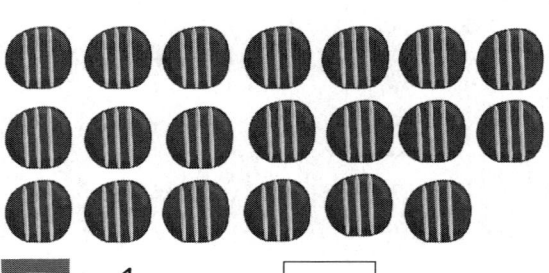 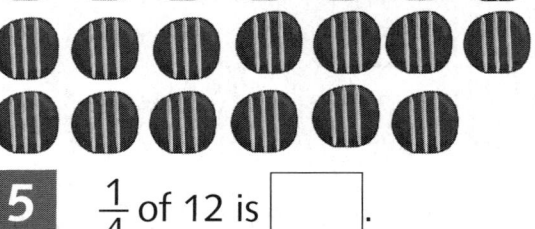

2 1 mark

3 1 mark

4 Quarter of 16 is ☐.

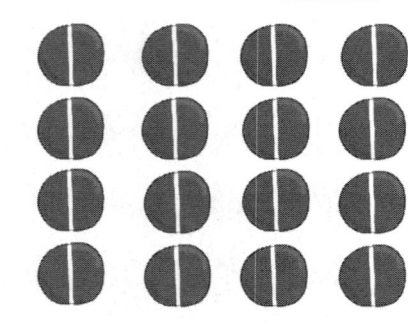

5 $\frac{1}{4}$ of 12 is ☐.

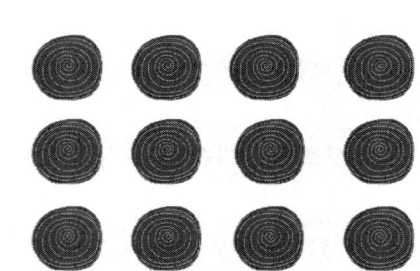 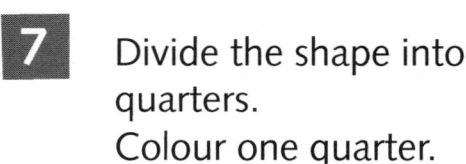

4 1 mark

5 1 mark

6 Divide the shape into quarters. Colour one quarter.

7 Divide the shape into quarters. Colour one quarter.

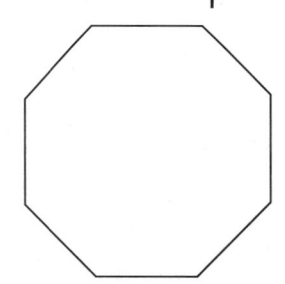

6 1 mark

7 1 mark

8 8 orange quarters. How many whole oranges? ☐

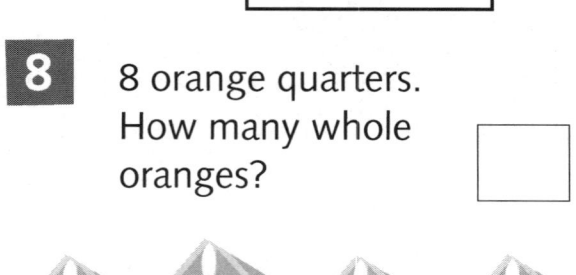

9 12 orange quarters. How many whole oranges? ☐

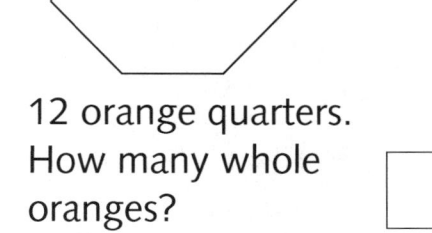 

8 1 mark

9 1 mark

Year 1 | Unit 8 | Week 2: Fractions   Total: ☐ out of 10   Mastery: NYA A A&E

1 Circle the container that is **half full**.

2 Circle the container that is **full**.

1
1 mark

2
1 mark

3 Circle the container that is **quarter full**.

4 Circle the container that is **empty**.

3
1 mark

4
1 mark

5 Circle the two objects that hold **less** than 1 litre.

6 Circle the two objects that hold **more** than 1 litre.

5
2 marks

6
2 marks

7 Circle the jug with the **greatest** capacity.

8 Show this jug with 1 litre of water in it.

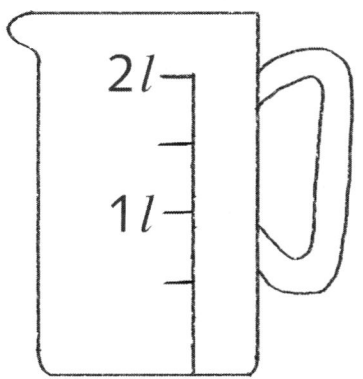

7
1 mark

8
1 mark

Name: _____ Date: _____

1 Write each number in numerals.

a) sixteen ☐ **b)** nineteen ☐

c) twelve ☐ **d)** fifteen ☐

1
4 marks

2 Show the value of each digit in these numbers. The first one has been done for you.

25   **a)**   28   **b)**   14   **c)**   36   **d)**   29

| 20 | 5 | ☐ | ☐ | ☐ | ☐ | ☐ | ☐ | ☐ | ☐ |

2
4 marks

3 **a)** How many balls? **b)** How many balls?

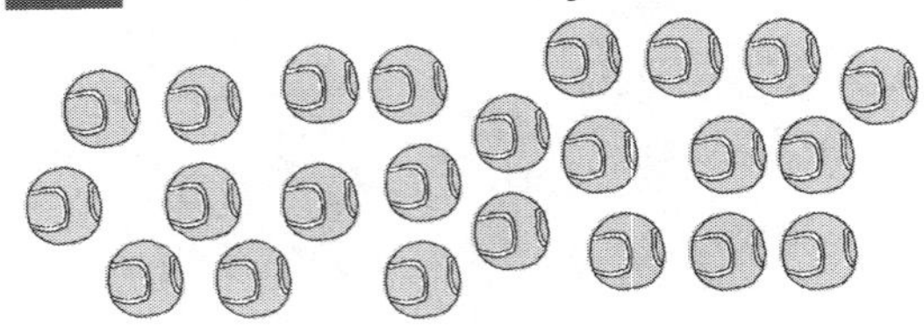

☐

☐

c) How many balls? **d)** How many balls?

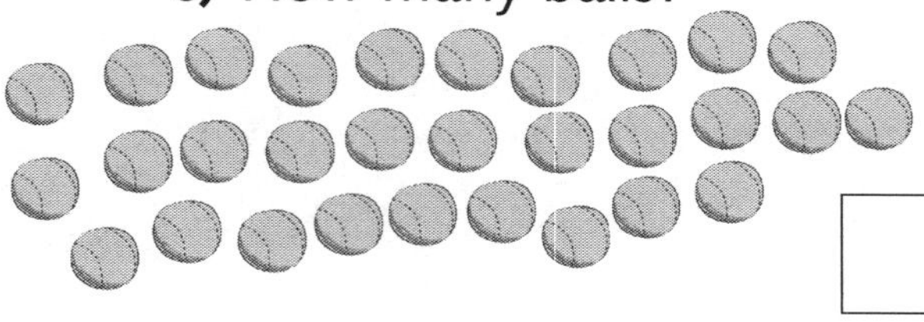

☐

☐

3
4 marks

4 Continue each number pattern.

a) 2, 4, 6, 8, ☐, 12, 14, ☐

b) 1, 3, 5, ☐, 9, 11, ☐, 15

c) 7, 12, 17, 22, ☐, 32, 37, ☐

d) 24, ☐, 44, 54, 64, ☐, 84, 94

e) 27, 25, ☐, 21, 19, ☐, 15, 13

f) 1, 11, ☐, 31, 41, 51, 61, ☐

g) 91, 81, ☐, 61, ☐, 41, 31, 21

h) 32, 27, 22, 17, ☐, ☐, 2

4
8 marks

Total: ☐ out of 20 Mastery: NYA A A&E

1 Double each of these numbers.

a) 4 ☐   b) 6 ☐   c) 3 ☐   d) 5 ☐

1
4 marks

2 a) 8 + 8 = ☐   b) 7 + 7 = ☐

c) 10 + 10 = ☐   d) 9 + 9 = ☐

2
4 marks

3 a) 7 + 8 = ☐   b) 9 + 10 = ☐

c) 8 + 9 = ☐   d) 6 + 7 = ☐

3
4 marks

4 a) 3 + 4 + 2 = ☐   b) 5 + 2 + 7 = ☐

c) 8 + 2 + 3 = ☐   d) 2 + 6 + 4 = ☐

4
4 marks

5 Use each set of three numbers to make an addition and a subtraction number fact.

a)

b)

☐ + ☐ = ☐   ☐ + ☐ = ☐

☐ − ☐ = ☐   ☐ − ☐ = ☐

5
4 marks

1 Listen carefully.

1
7 marks

2 a) A boy is facing his computer. He makes **one quarter turn** to the **right**. Colour what he is now facing.

b) The boy is facing his computer. He makes **one half turn**. Circle what he is now facing.

c) The boy is facing his computer. He makes a **three-quarter turn** to the **right**. Draw a cross (✗) on what he is now facing.

2
3 marks

You will need:
• coloured pencil

1 Continue each number pattern.

a) 0, 2, ☐, 6, 8, 10, ☐

b) 0, 5, 10, ☐, ☐, 25

c) 0, 10, ☐, 30, ☐, 50

d) 20, 22, ☐, 26, 28, ☐

e) 50, ☐, 40, 35, ☐, 25

f) 24, 26, ☐, 30, ☐, 34

g) 90, 80, ☐, ☐, 50, 40

h) 25, 30, ☐, 40, 45, ☐

1
8 marks

2 **a)** 7 lots of 2 is ☐.

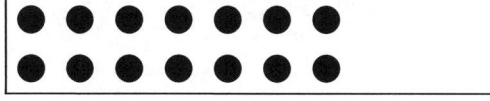

b) 5 lots of 2 is ☐.

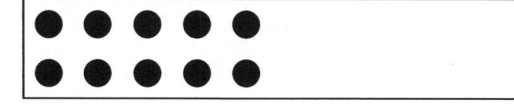

c) 9 lots of 2 is ☐.

d) 3 lots of 2 is ☐.

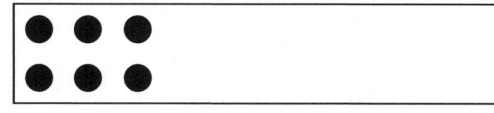

2
4 marks

3 Colour the stars to show the array.
Then complete the statement.

a) An array of 20 stars.

☆ ☆ ☆ ☆ ☆ ☆ ☆ ☆ ☆ ☆
☆ ☆ ☆ ☆ ☆ ☆ ☆ ☆ ☆ ☆
☆ ☆ ☆ ☆ ☆ ☆ ☆ ☆ ☆ ☆
☆ ☆ ☆ ☆ ☆ ☆ ☆ ☆ ☆ ☆
☆ ☆ ☆ ☆ ☆ ☆ ☆ ☆ ☆ ☆

☐ lots of ☐ is 20.

b) An array of 15 stars.

☆ ☆ ☆ ☆ ☆ ☆ ☆ ☆ ☆ ☆
☆ ☆ ☆ ☆ ☆ ☆ ☆ ☆ ☆ ☆
☆ ☆ ☆ ☆ ☆ ☆ ☆ ☆ ☆ ☆

☐ lots of ☐ is 15.

c) An array of 25 stars.

☆ ☆ ☆ ☆ ☆ ☆ ☆ ☆ ☆ ☆
☆ ☆ ☆ ☆ ☆ ☆ ☆ ☆ ☆ ☆
☆ ☆ ☆ ☆ ☆ ☆ ☆ ☆ ☆ ☆
☆ ☆ ☆ ☆ ☆ ☆ ☆ ☆ ☆ ☆
☆ ☆ ☆ ☆ ☆ ☆ ☆ ☆ ☆ ☆

☐ lots of ☐ is 25.

d) An array of 30 stars.

☆ ☆ ☆ ☆ ☆ ☆ ☆ ☆ ☆ ☆
☆ ☆ ☆ ☆ ☆ ☆ ☆ ☆ ☆ ☆
☆ ☆ ☆ ☆ ☆ ☆ ☆ ☆ ☆ ☆
☆ ☆ ☆ ☆ ☆ ☆ ☆ ☆ ☆ ☆
☆ ☆ ☆ ☆ ☆ ☆ ☆ ☆ ☆ ☆

☐ lots of ☐ is 30.

3
8 marks

1 a) ☐ bikes. Each bike has ☐ wheels.

That's ☐ wheels altogether.

b) ☐ feet. Each foot has ☐ toes.

That's ☐ toes altogether.

c) ☐ clowns. Each clown has ☐ balloons.

That's ☐ balloons altogether.

1
3 marks

2 a) ☐ shared between ☐ is ☐ .

b) ☐ shared between ☐ is ☐ .

c) ☐ shared between ☐ is ☐ .

2
3 marks

3 a) There are 10 skittles in a set. How many skittles altogether in 5 sets? ☐

b) Each bag holds 6 cricket stumps. How many bags are needed for 30 stumps? ☐

c) Each tube holds 4 tennis balls. How many tubes are needed for 20 balls? ☐

d) Each bag holds 5 footballs. How many footballs in 7 bags? ☐

3
4 marks

1 Circle the objects that are **shorter** than a 30 centimetre ruler.

1
2 marks

2 Circle the objects that are **longer** than a 1 metre rule.

2
2 marks

3 Draw lines to show the pairs of branches that would balance.

3
4 marks

4  weighs 5 blocks. weighs 7 blocks.  weighs 10 blocks.

How many blocks would be needed to balance each pan balance?

a)

b)

4
2 marks

1 a) 18 − 7 = ☐ b) 8 + 11 = ☐

c) 16 − 9 = ☐ d) 12 + 5 = ☐

e) 4 + 16 = ☐ f) 20 − 11 = ☐

1
6 marks

2 a) 10 + 8 = ☐ b) 17 − 4 = ☐

11 + ☐ = 18 17 − ☐ = 12

12 + ☐ = 18 17 − 6 = ☐

2
6 marks

3 a) 5 adults and 11 children go on a picnic. How many people go on the picnic? b) 18 people go mountain climbing. 7 are children and the rest are adults. How many adults go mountain climbing?

☐ ○ ☐ ○ ☐ ☐ ○ ☐ ○ ☐

3
4 marks

4 a) Simon has 20 p. He gives 5 p to Jacob. How much does Simon have left?

☐ p ○ ☐ p ○ ☐ p

b) Amy has 13 p. She finds a 5 p coin in the sofa. How much does Amy have now?

☐ p ○ ☐ p ○ ☐ p

4
4 marks

Year 1 | Unit 11 | Week 1: Addition and subtraction   Total: ☐ out of 20 Mastery: NYA A A&E

1

a) 12 p + 2 p = ☐ p

b) 16 p − 5 p = ☐ p

c) 15 p − 9 p = ☐ p

d) 13 p + 5 p = ☐ p

e) 11 p + 7 p = ☐ p

f) 20 p − 10 p = ☐ p

1
6 marks

2

a) 12 − 10 = ☐

b) 7 + 10 = ☐

c) 18 − 10 = ☐

d) 5 + 10 = ☐

e) 9 + 10 = ☐

f) 15 − 10 = ☐

2
6 marks

3 Use the three numbers to make two addition and two subtraction number facts.

☐ + ☐ = ☐   ☐ + ☐ = ☐

☐ − ☐ = ☐   ☐ − ☐ = ☐

3
4 marks

4

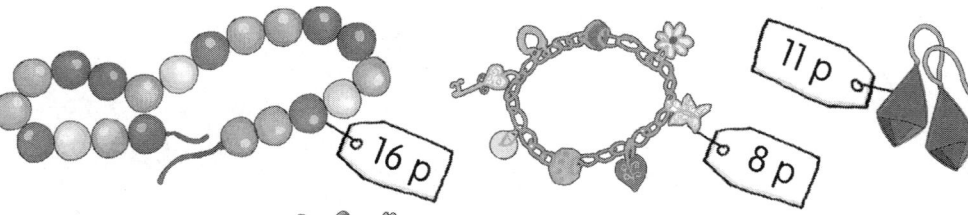

a) Ruby buys a  and a . How much does Ruby spend?

☐ p ◯ ☐ p ◯ ☐ p

b) Jules has 20 p. She buys a 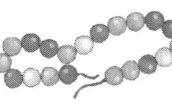 . How much does Jules have left?

☐ p ◯ ☐ p ◯ ☐ p

4
4 marks

Name: _____ Date: _____

1 Continue each pattern.

a)
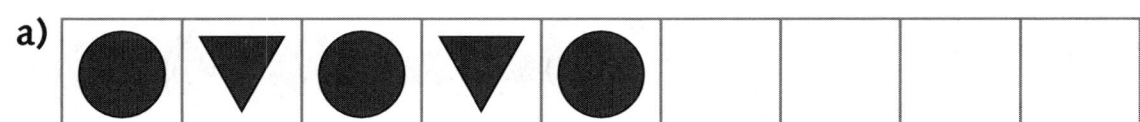

b)

c)

d)

1
4 marks

2 Draw lines to match each object to the name of its shape.

triangle

sphere

cube

square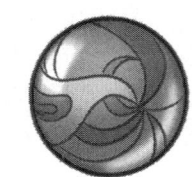

cylinder

cone

2
6 marks

1 Double each of these numbers.

    a) 5 ☐   **b)** 8 ☐   **c)** 7 ☐   **1**

3 marks

2 Halve each of these numbers.

    a) 20 ☐   **b)** 12 ☐   **c)** 18 ☐   **2**

3 marks

3 Circle one quarter of each bunch of grapes.

    a)   **b)**

    One quarter of 12 is ☐ .   One quarter of 16 is ☐ .

    c)   **d)**

    One quarter of 20 is ☐ .   One quarter of 24 is ☐ .   **3**

8 marks

4 **a)** Harry had 8 chocolates.
        He ate one quarter of them.
        How many chocolates did Harry eat? ☐

    b) Jay had 14 sweets.
        His sister only had half as many sweets.
        How many sweets did Jay's sister have? ☐

    b) Sally had 10 biscuits.
        Her sister had double that number of biscuits.
        How many biscuits did Sally's sister have? ☐   **4**

6 marks

1 Divide the shape in half. Colour **one half**.

2 Divide the shape into quarters. Colour **one quarter**.

You will need:
• ruler
• coloured pencil

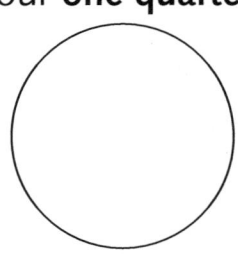

| | 1 |
| 1 mark |
| | 2 |
| 1 mark |

3 Divide the shape into quarters. Colour **three quarters**.

4 Divide the shape in quarters. Colour **one half**.

| | 3 |
| 1 mark |
| | 4 |
| 1 mark |

5 $\frac{1}{2}$ of 18 is ☐ .

6 $\frac{1}{4}$ of 20 is ☐ .

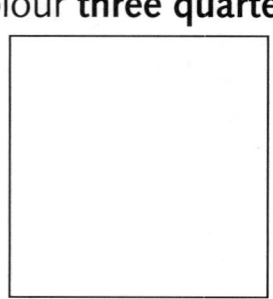

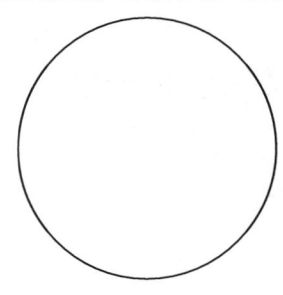

| | 5 |
| 1 mark |
| | 6 |
| 1 mark |

7 **a)** $\frac{1}{2}$ of 24 is ☐ .   **b)** $\frac{1}{4}$ of 24 is ☐ .

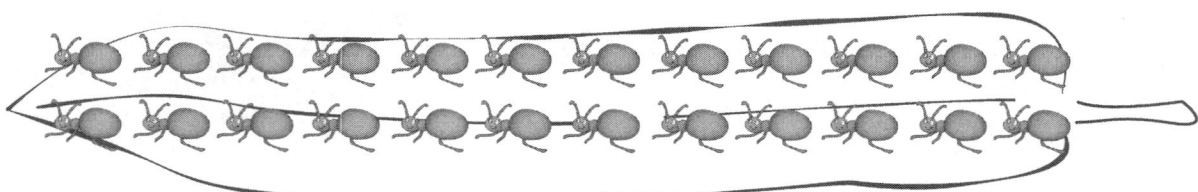

| | 7 |
| 2 marks |

8 10 apple halves. How many whole apples?

9 12 apple quarters. How many whole apples?

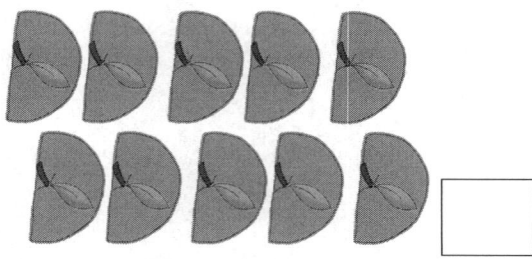
☐

☐

| | 8 |
| 1 mark |
| | 9 |
| 1 mark |

1 Read the time on the first clock.
Then draw hands on the second clock to show the new time.

a) 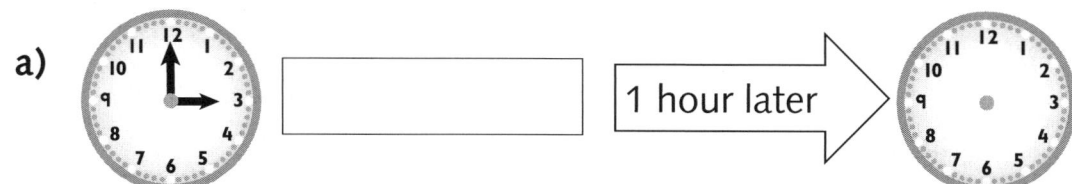 1 hour later

b) 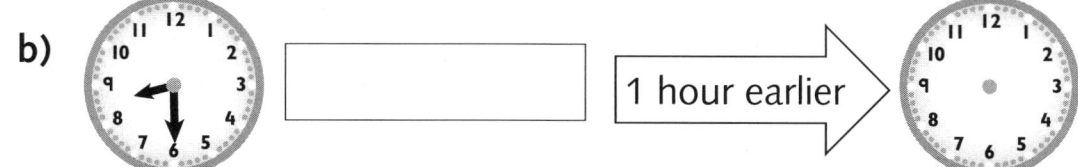 1 hour earlier

c) 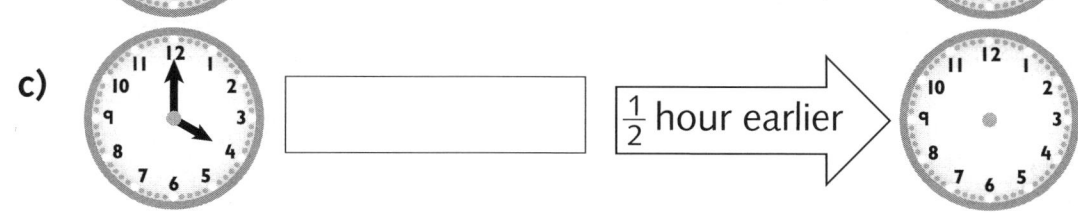 $\frac{1}{2}$ hour earlier

1
6 marks

2 How many hours have passed between each pair of clocks?

a)    hours

b)    hours

c)    hours

2
3 marks

3 Draw lines to match each amount of time to the picture of something that takes about that long.

| hour | minute | second |

Achoo!

3
1 mark

Year 1 | Unit 12 | Week 3: Measurement (time)   Total: ____ out of 10   Mastery: NYA   A   A&E

Year 1 End-of-unit Tests — Notes, oral questions, answers and marking commentary

Unit 1

Week 1: Number – Number and place value

1 a) 5, 6   b) 16, 17

2 a) 10   b) 13

3 a) 17   b) 10

4 a) 12   b) 17

5 7th and 12th shells circled

Week 2: Number – Addition and subtraction

1 a) 2 + 1 = 3   b) 2 + 2 = 4

2 a) 5   b) 4

3 a) 5 – 2 = 3   b) 3 – 2 = 1

4 a) 2   b) 1

5 a) 1   b) 3

Week 3: Geometry – Properties of shapes

1 a) Both circles coloured
   b) Tick inside all 3 squares
   c) All 4 rectangles circled
   d) A cross inside all 5 triangles

2 a) 4   b) 3   c) 1

3 a) 4   b) 0   c) 3

Unit 2

Week 1: Number – Addition and subtraction

1 a) 8   b) 6   c) 7   d) 9

2 a) 6   b) 1   c) 2   d) 6

3 a) 4   b) 10   c) 6

4   3 + 2 = 5 → 5 – 3 = 2
    6 + 4 = 10 → 10 – 6 = 4
    2 + 5 = 7 → 7 – 2 = 5

Week 2: Number: Addition and subtraction

1 a) 5 + 4 = 9 → 4 + 5 = 9
   b) 7 + 3 = 10 → 3 + 7 = 10
   c) 6 + 2 = 8 → 2 + 6 = 8

2 a) 5   b) 3

3 a) 4   b) 4   c) 5
   d) 5   e) 10

4 Award 2 marks per question for the correct answer. If the answer is incorrect, award 1 mark for identifying the correct calculation.
   a) 6 – 2 = 4   b) 3 + 5 = 8

Week 3: Measurement (length and height)

1 Longest ribbon circled

2 Shortest rope circled

3 Tallest tree circled

4 Shortest flagpole circle

5 a) 14 cm   b) 9 cm   c) 5 cm

6 a) 10 cm line drawn
   b) 13 cm line drawn

7 A line shorter than 8 cm drawn

Unit 3

Week 1: Number – Number and place value

1   8, 10

2   20, 25

3   40, 50

4   30, 45

5   12, 16

6   70, 90

7   14, 8

8   20, 10

9   50, 20

10   22, 28

Week 2: Number – Multiplication and division

Q1–5: For each question:
- Award 1 mark per question for the correct answer to parts a and b.
- Award 1 mark per question for the correct answer to part c.

1 a) 5   b) 2   c) 10

2 a) 4   b) 5   c) 20

3 a) 3   b) 10   c) 30

4 a) 7   b) 2   c) 14

5 a) 5   b) 5   c) 25

Week 3: Geometry – Position and direction

1 Cup to the right of the bowl circled

2 Glass to the left of the jug circled

3 a) Mixing bowl drawn below flour
   b) Tea container drawn above rice
   c) Wooden spoon drawn between flour and rice

4 a)   b) 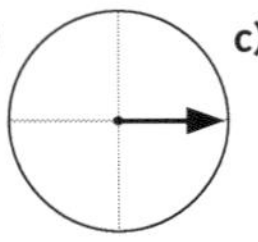   c)

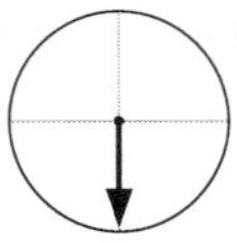

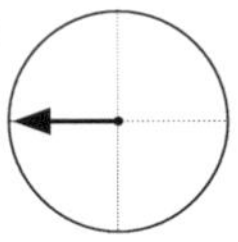

5 a) The toy box coloured
   b) Sideboard circled

Unit 4

Week 1: Number – Addition and subtraction

1 a) 11   b) 12   c) 13
   d) 13   e) 15   f) 14

2 a) 7   b) 9   c) 3
   d) 8   e) 11   f) 3

3 a) 5   b) 8   c) 6
   d) 8

4 Award 2 marks per question for the correct answer. If the answer is incorrect, award 1 mark for identifying the correct calculation.
   a) 5 + 7 = 12   b) 13 – 4 = 9

Week 2: Number – Fractions

1 Square and triangle circled

2 3 apples circled

3 4 cm

4 2

5 6

6 Line dividing pear in half; half coloured

7 Line dividing pineapple in half; half coloured

8 4

9 6

Week 3: Measurement (money)

1   1 x 10 p → 2 x 5 p
    1 x 20 p → 2 x 10 p
    1 x 5 p → 5 x 1 p
    1 x 2 p → 2 x 1 p

2 a) Drawing of coins totalling 8 p
   b) Drawing of coins totalling 11 p

3 a) 7 p; 3 p change
   b) 9 p; 1 p change

Unit 5

Week 1: Number – Number and place value

1 a) 5, 6, 7, 8
   b) 9, 12, 14, 18
   c) 8, 10, 13, 17
   d) 11, 14, 16, 19

2 8, 14, 16, 20 circled

3 3, 9, 15, 17 circled

4 a) 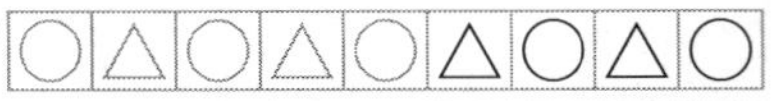
   b) 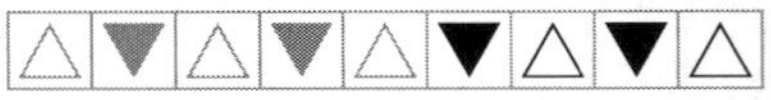
   c) 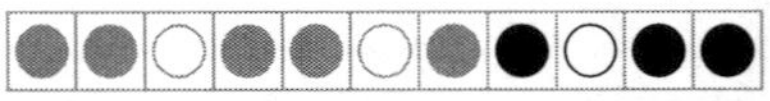
   d)

Week 2: Number – Addition and subtraction, including Measurement (money)

1 a) 4 p   b) 3 p

2 a) 6 p + 2 p = 8 p
   b) 4 p + 6 p = 10 p

3 a) Coins circled totalling 9 p
   b) Coins circled totalling 6 p

4 Award 2 marks per question for the correct answer. If the answer is incorrect, award 1 mark for identifying the correct calculation.
   a) 12 p – 10 p = 2 p
   b) 8 p + 6 p = 14 p

Week 3: Geometry – Properties of shapes

1 All the shapes matched to the correct name

2 4 cubes circled

3 Square, circle, triangle and rectangle circled

Unit 6

Week 1: Number – Multiplication and division, including Number and place value

1 a) 20, 25 **b)** 16, 24 **c)** 40, 70
   d) 24, 18 **e)** 30, 50 **f)** 80, 50

2 a) 40   **b)** 30   **c)** 16   **d)** 25

Week 2: Number – Multiplication and division

1 a) 3 sets of 5 make 15 altogether.
   b) 5 sets of 10 make 50 altogether.
   c) 7 sets of 2 make 14 altogether.

2 a) 8 shared between 2 is 4.
   b) 6 shared between 3 is 2.
   c) 12 shared between 4 is 3.

3 a) 3   **b)** 20   **c)** 30   **d)** 6

Week 3: Measurement (mass)

1 Loaf of bread circled

2 Watering can circled

3 Sofa circled

4 Newspaper circled

5 Watermelon circled

6 Smaller quantity of cherries circled

7 a) 7 kg   **b)** 3 kg   **c)** 4 kg   **d)** 5 kg

Unit 7

Week 1: Number – Addition and subtraction

1 a) 7   **b)** 8   **c)** 6   **d)** 5

2 a) 7   **b)** 9   **c)** 5   **d)** 11

3 $6 + 3 = 9 \rightarrow 9 - 6 = 3$
   $2 + 4 = 6 \rightarrow 6 - 2 = 4$
   $7 + 1 = 8 \rightarrow 8 - 7 = 1$
   $8 + 2 = 10 \rightarrow 10 - 8 = 2$

Week 2: Number – Addition and subtraction

1 a) $7 + 5 = 12$ **b)** $6 + 8 = 14$
   c) $11 + 3 = 14$ **d)** $5 + 10 = 15$

2 a) $13 - 8 = 5$ **b)** $12 - 4 = 8$
   c) $15 - 7 = 8$ **d)** $14 - 5 = 9$

3 a) 6   **b)** 4   **c)** 3
   d) 6   **e)** 4   **f)** 9

4 a) 5   **b)** 4   **c)** 7
   d) 10   **e)** 1   **f)** 10

Week 3: Measurement (time)

1 a) The day before Wednesday → Tuesday
   b) The day after Friday → Saturday

2 a) The month before June → May
   b) The month after February → March

3 a) Summer circled

4

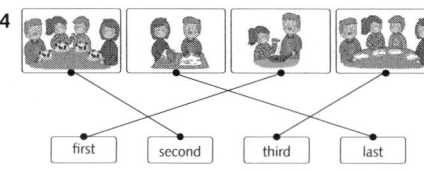

first   second   third   last

5 a) 2:00 or 2 o'clock
   b) 7:30 or half past 7

6 a)   **b)**

Unit 8

Week 1: Number – Number and place value

1 a) four   **b)** seven   **c)** five   **d)** eight

2 $14 \rightarrow 10 + 4$
   $20 \rightarrow 10 + 10$
   $11 \rightarrow 10 + 1$
   $17 \rightarrow 10 + 7$

3 a) 16   **b)** 9   **c)** 20

4 a) 5   **b)** 17   **c)** 10

5 7, 10, 15, 18

6 a) 17   **b)** 19

7 a) 6 and 18 circled
   b) 15 and 30 circled
   c) 20 and 40 circled

Week 2: Number – Fractions

1 Rectangle and circle circled

2 2 buttons circled

3 5 buttons circled

4 4

5 3

6 Square divided into quarters; 1 quarter coloured

7 Octagon divided into quarters; 1 quarter coloured

8 2

9 3

Week 3: Measurement (volume and capacity)

1 Glass circled

2 Bucket circled

3 Jug circled

4 Jug circled

5 Cup and glass circled

6 Kitchen sink and swimming pool circled

7 Largest jug circled

8 Jug shown as filled to 1 litre mark

Unit 9

Week 1: Number – Number and place value

1 a) 16   **b)** 19   **c)** 12   **d)** 15

2 a) 20, 8   **b)** 10, 4   **c)** 30, 6   **d)** 20, 9

3 a) 23   **b)** 27   **c)** 30   **d)** 25

4 a) 10, 16 **b)** 7, 13   **c)** 27, 42 **d)** 34, 74
   e) 23, 17 **f)** 21, 71 **g)** 71, 51 **h)** 12, 7

Week 2: Number – Position and direction

1 a) 8   **b)** 12   **c)** 6   **d)** 10

2 a) 16   **b)** 14   **c)** 20   **d)** 18

3 a) 15   **b)** 19   **c)** 17   **d)** 13

4 a) 9   **b)** 14   **c)** 13   **d)** 12

5 a) $4 + 8 = 12$ OR $8 + 4 = 12$; $12 - 8 = 4$ or $12 - 4 = 8$
   b) $6 + 9 = 15$ OR $9 + 6 = 15$; $15 - 9 = 6$ or $15 - 6 = 9$

Week 3: Geometry – Position and direction

Oral questions

1 *Look at the picture of the table and chairs.*
   a) *Colour the chair on the* **right**.
   b) *Draw a glass* **on** *the table.*
   c) *Draw a cat* **underneath** *the table.*
   d) *Draw a tree* **between** *the table and chairs and the flowerbed.*
   e) *Draw a bird standing* **on top of** *the umbrella.*
   f) *Draw some clouds* **above** *the umbrella.*
   g) *Draw a person standing* **behind** *the chair on the* **left**.

1 a) Chair on the right coloured
   b) A glass drawn on the table
   c) A cat drawn beneath the table
   d) A tree drawn between the right hand chair and the flower bed
   e) A bird drawn on top of the umbrella
   f) Clouds drawn above the umbrella
   g) A person drawn standing behind the chair on the left

2 a) Window coloured
   b) Chest of drawers circled
   c) Cross drawn on book shelf

Unit 10

Week 1: Number – Multiplication and division, including Number and place value

1 a) 4, 12   **b)** 15, 20   **c)** 20, 40   **d)** 24, 30
   e) 45, 30   **f)** 28, 32   **g)** 70, 60   **h)** 35, 50

2 a) 14   **b)** 10   **c)** 18   **d)** 6

3 a) An array of 20 stars coloured;
     a statement to match the array
     coloured, e.g. 2 lots of 10 is 20 or
     4 lots of 5 is 20.
   b) An array of 15 stars coloured;
     a statement to match the array
     coloured, e.g. 3 lots of 5 is 15.
   c) An array of 25 stars coloured;
     5 lots of 5 is 25.
   d) An array of 30 stars coloured;
     a statement to match the array
     coloured, e.g. 3 lots of 10 is 30 or
     5 lots of 6 is 30.

Week 2: Number – Multiplication and division

1 a) 4 bikes. Each bike has 2 wheels.
     That's 8 wheels altogether.
   b) 6 feet. Each foot has 5 toes.
     That's 30 toes altogether.
   c) 8 clowns. Each clown has 10 balloons.
     That's 80 balloons altogether.

2 a) 9 shared between 3 is 3
   b) 12 shared between 2 is 6
   c) 16 shared between 4 is 4

3 a) 50   **b)** 5   **c)** 5   **d)** 35

Week 3: Measurement

1 Leaf and pencil circled

2 Skipping rope and boat circled

3
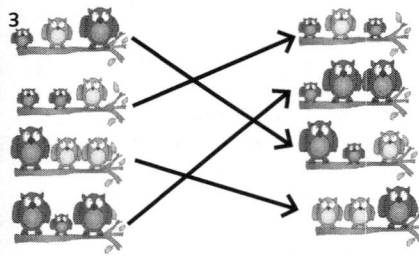

4 a) 15 blocks   **b)** 12 blocks

Unit 11

Week 1: Number – Addition and subtraction

Q3–4: For each question:
- Award 2 marks for each part for the correct answer.
- If the answer is incorrect, award 1 mark for identifying the correct calculation.

1 a) 11   **b)** 19   **c)** 7
   d) 17   **e)** 20   **f)** 9

2 a) 18, 7, 6   **b)** 13, 5, 11

3 a) 5 + 11 = 16   **b)** 18 − 7 = 11

4 a) 20 p − 5 p = 15 p   **b)** 13 p + 5 p = 18 p

Week 2: Number – Addition and subtraction

1 a) 14 p   **b)** 11 p   **c)** 6 p
   d) 18 p   **e)** 18 p   **f)** 10 p

2 a) 2   **b)** 17   **c)** 8
   d) 15   **e)** 19   **f)** 5

3 7 + 8 = 15
   8 + 7 = 15
   15 − 8 = 7
   15 − 7 = 8

4 Award 2 marks per question for the correct answer. If the answer is incorrect, award 1 mark for identifying the correct calculation.
   a) 8 + 11 = 19   **b)** 20 − 16 = 4

Week 3: Geometry – Properties of shapes

1 a)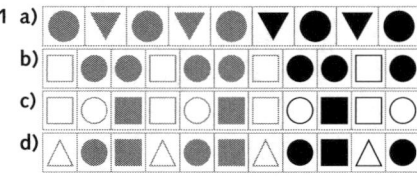
   b)
   c)
   d)

2
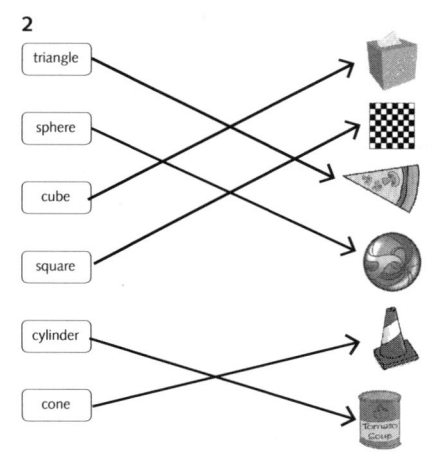

triangle   sphere   cube   square   cylinder   cone

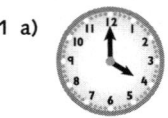  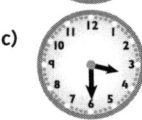

Unit 12

Week 1: Number – Multiplication and division

1 a) 10   **b)** 16   **c)** 14

2 a) 10   **b)** 6   **c)** 9

3 a) 3 grapes circled; One quarter of 12 is 3.
   b) 4 grapes circled; One quarter of 16 is 4.
   c) 5 grapes circled; One quarter of 20 is 5.
   d) 6 grapes circled; One quarter of 24 is 6.

4 Award 2 marks per question for the correct answer. If the answer is incorrect, award 1 mark for evidence of working out.
   a) 2   **b)** 7   **c)** 20

Week 2: Number – Fractions

1 Square divided in half; 1 half coloured

2 Circle divided into quarters; 1 quarter coloured

3 Square divided into quarters; 3 quarters coloured

4 Circle divided into quarters; 2 quarters coloured

5 9

6 5

7 a) 12   **b)** 6

8 5

9 3

Week 3: Measurement (time)

1 a)
   b)
   c)

2 a) 3 hours
   b) 4 hours
   c) $2\frac{1}{2}$ hours

3

hour	minute	second

My record sheet

Year 1
Unit 1

Name: _____

Date: _____

Week 3 — 2-D shapes

	Start of the week	End of the week
• I can recognise and name a circle, triangle, rectangle and square	☺ 😐 ☹	☺ 😐 ☹
• I can recognise different triangles	☺ 😐 ☹	☺ 😐 ☹
• I know the difference between a rectangle and a square	☺ 😐 ☹	☺ 😐 ☹

	Start of the week	End of the week
• I can join two groups of objects and count how many there are altogether	😊 😐 ☹️	😊 😐 ☹️
• I can write an addition number sentence	😊 😐 ☹️	😊 😐 ☹️
• I can work out an addition number sentence by counting on	😊 😐 ☹️	😊 😐 ☹️
• I can take away a small group of objects from a larger group and count how many are left	😊 😐 ☹️	😊 😐 ☹️
• I can write a subtraction number sentence	😊 😐 ☹️	😊 😐 ☹️
• I can work out a subtraction number sentence by counting back	😊 😐 ☹️	😊 😐 ☹️

	Start of the week	End of the week
• I can read and write numbers to 20	😊 😐 ☹️	😊 😐 ☹️
• I can count up to 20 objects	😊 😐 ☹️	😊 😐 ☹️
• I can say the number that is 1 more or 1 less than another number	😊 😐 ☹️	😊 😐 ☹️
• I can put things in order from 1st to 20th	😊 😐 ☹️	😊 😐 ☹️

My record sheet

Year 1
Unit 2

Name: _____

Date: _____

Week 3 — Length and height

	Start of the week	End of the week
• I can talk about and compare lengths	😊 😐 😞	😊 😐 😞
• I can talk about and compare heights	😊 😐 😞	😊 😐 😞
• I understand the difference between length, height and width	😊 😐 😞	😊 😐 😞
• I can measure objects using my hands and feet	😊 😐 😞	😊 😐 😞
• I know that 'centimetres' can be used to measure length and height	😊 😐 😞	😊 😐 😞
• I can use a ruler	😊 😐 😞	😊 😐 😞

Week 2 — Addition and subtraction

	Start of the week	End of the week
• I know that addition can be done in any order	☺ 😐 ☹	☺ 😐 ☹
• I can find the difference between two numbers	☺ 😐 ☹	☺ 😐 ☹
• I can solve missing number problems such as 3 + ☐ = 7	☺ 😐 ☹	☺ 😐 ☹
• I can solve addition and subtraction problems	☺ 😐 ☹	☺ 😐 ☹

Week 1 — Addition and subtraction

	Start of the week	End of the week
• I can recall addition facts to 10	☺ 😐 ☹	☺ 😐 ☹
• I can recall subtraction facts to 10	☺ 😐 ☹	☺ 😐 ☹
• I can recall addition doubles to 5 + 5	☺ 😐 ☹	☺ 😐 ☹
• I know how addition and subtraction facts such as 3 + 1 = 4 and 4 − 3 = 1 are related	☺ 😐 ☹	☺ 😐 ☹

My record sheet

Year 1
Unit 3

Name: _____

Date: _____

Week 3 — Position and direction

	Start of the week	End of the week
• I can use words such as 'up', 'down', 'left' and 'right' to talk about direction	☺ 😐 ☹	☺ 😐 ☹
• I can use words such as 'above', 'below' and 'between' to talk about position	☺ 😐 ☹	☺ 😐 ☹
• I can talk about and make whole and half turns	☺ 😐 ☹	☺ 😐 ☹
• I can talk about and make quarter and three-quarter turns	☺ 😐 ☹	☺ 😐 ☹

	Start of the week	End of the week
• I can count on or back in steps of 2	🙂 😐 ☹	🙂 😐 ☹
• I can count on or back in steps of 5	🙂 😐 ☹	🙂 😐 ☹
• I can count on or back in steps of 10	🙂 😐 ☹	🙂 😐 ☹

	Start of the week	End of the week
• I can count a group of objects in 2s and work out how many there are altogether	🙂 😐 ☹	🙂 😐 ☹
• I can count a group of objects in 5s and work out how many there are altogether	🙂 😐 ☹	🙂 😐 ☹
• I can count a group of objects in 10s and work out how many there are altogether	🙂 😐 ☹	🙂 😐 ☹
• I can share a group of objects into equal sets	🙂 😐 ☹	🙂 😐 ☹

My record sheet

Year 1
Unit 4

Name: _____

Date: _____

Week 3 — Money

	Start of the week	End of the week
• I can recognise different coins	😊 😐 😞	😊 😐 😞
• I can use coins to show different ways of making the same total	😊 😐 😞	😊 😐 😞
• I can find totals using money	😊 😐 😞	😊 😐 😞
• I can give change	😊 😐 😞	😊 😐 😞

	Start of the week	End of the week
• I can find half of a shape	☺ 😐 ☹	☺ 😐 ☹
• I can find half of a set of objects	☺ 😐 ☹	☺ 😐 ☹
• I can find half of a length	☺ 😐 ☹	☺ 😐 ☹
• I can join two halves to make one whole	☺ 😐 ☹	☺ 😐 ☹

	Start of the week	End of the week
• I can recall addition facts to 15	☺ 😐 ☹	☺ 😐 ☹
• I can recall subtraction facts to 15	☺ 😐 ☹	☺ 😐 ☹
• I can solve missing number problems such as $8 - \boxed{} = 3$	☺ 😐 ☹	☺ 😐 ☹
• I can solve addition and subtraction problems	☺ 😐 ☹	☺ 😐 ☹

My record sheet

Year 1
Unit 5

Name: _____

Date: _____

	Start of the week	End of the week
• I can recognise and name common 3-D shapes	🙂 🙂 ☹️	🙂 🙂 ☹️
• I know the difference between a cube and a cuboid	🙂 🙂 ☹️	🙂 🙂 ☹️
• I can sort 2-D and 3-D shapes	🙂 🙂 ☹️	🙂 🙂 ☹️

Week 1 — Number

	Start of the week	End of the week
I can say the number that is 1 more or 1 less than another number	😊 😐 😞	😊 😐 😞
I can order numbers to 20	😊 😐 😞	😊 😐 😞
I can count on in 2s from 0 and 1	😊 😐 😞	😊 😐 😞
I know odd and even numbers to 20	😊 😐 😞	😊 😐 😞
I can spot a pattern and continue it	😊 😐 😞	😊 😐 😞

Week 2 — Addition and subtraction, including Money

	Start of the week	End of the week
I can find totals using money	😊 😐 😞	😊 😐 😞
I can give change	😊 😐 😞	😊 😐 😞
I can write an addition number sentence involving money	😊 😐 😞	😊 😐 😞
I can write a subtraction number sentence involving money	😊 😐 😞	😊 😐 😞
I can solve addition and subtraction problems involving money	😊 😐 😞	😊 😐 😞

My record sheet

Year 1
Unit 6

Name: _____

Date: _____

Week 3 — Weight

	Start of the week	End of the week
• I can talk about and compare weights	😊 🙂 ☹️	☹️ 🙂 ☹️
• I can use a balance	😊 🙂 ☹️	☹️ 🙂 ☹️
• I know that 'kilograms' can be used to measure weight	😊 🙂 ☹️	☹️ 🙂 ☹️
• I can read a set of weighing scales	😊 🙂 ☹️	☹️ 🙂 ☹️

	Start of the week	End of the week
• I can count sets of 2, 5 or 10 and work out how many there are altogether	☺ 😐 ☹	☺ 😐 ☹
• I understand what the word 'multiplication' means	☺ 😐 ☹	☺ 😐 ☹
• I can share a group of objects into equal sets	☺ 😐 ☹	☺ 😐 ☹
• I understand what the word 'division' means	☺ 😐 ☹	☺ 😐 ☹
• I can solve grouping and sharing problems	☺ 😐 ☹	☺ 😐 ☹

	Start of the week	End of the week
• I can count on or back in steps of 2	☺ 😐 ☹	☺ 😐 ☹
• I can count on or back in steps of 5	☺ 😐 ☹	☺ 😐 ☹
• I can count on or back in steps of 10	☺ 😐 ☹	☺ 😐 ☹
• I can spot the missing number in a number pattern	☺ 😐 ☹	☺ 😐 ☹
• I can use a diagram to count in groups of 2, 5 or 10	☺ 😐 ☹	☺ 😐 ☹

My record sheet

Year 1
Unit 7

Name: _____

Date: _____

	Start of the week	End of the week
• I know the order of the days of the week	😊 😐 ☹️	😊 😐 ☹️
• I know the order of the months of the year	😊 😐 ☹️	😊 😐 ☹️
• I can order seasons of the year	😊 😐 ☹️	😊 😐 ☹️
• I can put events in order	😊 😐 ☹️	😊 😐 ☹️
• I can read and show o'clock times	😊 😐 ☹️	😊 😐 ☹️
• I can read and show half-past times	😊 😐 ☹️	😊 😐 ☹️

	Start of the week	End of the week
• I can use a number track to count on and back	🙂 ☹	🙂 😐 ☹
• I can work out an addition fact by counting on	🙂 ☹	🙂 😐 ☹
• I can work out a subtraction fact by counting back	🙂 ☹	🙂 😐 ☹
• I can write addition and subtraction number sentences	🙂 ☹	🙂 😐 ☹
• I can solve missing number problems such as $12 - \square = 5$	🙂 ☹	🙂 😐 ☹
• I can spot patterns in addition and subtraction facts	🙂 ☹	🙂 😐 ☹

	Start of the week	End of the week
• I know different pairs of numbers that add up to 10	🙂 ☹	🙂 😐 ☹
• I can recall addition doubles to $5 + 5$	🙂 ☹	🙂 😐 ☹
• I can use doubles to work out other addition facts	🙂 ☹	🙂 😐 ☹
• I can recall addition and subtraction facts to 10	🙂 ☹	🙂 😐 ☹
• I know how addition and subtraction facts such as $2 + 5 = 7$ and $7 - 5 = 2$ are related	🙂 ☹	🙂 😐 ☹

My record sheet

Year 1
Unit 8

Name: _____

Date: _____

Week 3 — Volume and capacity

	Start of the week	End of the week
• I can use words such as 'full', 'half full', 'quarter full' and 'empty'	☺ ☹	☺ ☹
• I can estimate and measure capacities	☺ ☹	☺ ☹
• I can compare and order capacities	☺ ☹	☺ ☹
• I know that 'litres' can be used to measure volume and capacity	☺ ☹	☺ ☹
• I can say if a container holds 'the same as', 'less than' or 'more than' a litre	☺ ☹	☺ ☹

Week 2 — Fractions

	Start of the week	End of the week
I can find one quarter of a shape	🙂 😐 / 😞	🙂 😐 / 😞
I can find one quarter of a set of objects	🙂 😐 / 😞	🙂 😐 / 😞
I can find one quarter of a length	🙂 😐 / 😞	🙂 😐 / 😞
I can join quarters to make one whole	🙂 😐 / 😞	🙂 😐 / 😞

Week 1 — Number and place value

	Start of the week	End of the week
I can read and write numbers to 10 in numerals (6) and in words (six)	🙂 😐 / 😞	🙂 😐 / 😞
I can say the number of 10s and 1s in a number to 20	🙂 😐 / 😞	🙂 😐 / 😞
I can compare two numbers saying which is 'more' or 'less'	🙂 😐 / 😞	🙂 😐 / 😞
I can say the number that is 1 more or 1 less than another number	🙂 😐 / 😞	🙂 😐 / 😞
I can order a set of numbers to 20	🙂 😐 / 😞	🙂 😐 / 😞
I can count to 100	🙂 😐 / 😞	🙂 😐 / 😞
I know different multiples of 2, 5 and 10	🙂 😐 / 😞	🙂 😐 / 😞

My record sheet

Year 1
Unit 9

Name: _____

Date: _____

Week 3 — Position and direction

	Start of the week	End of the week
• I can use words such as 'on top of', 'underneath', 'in front of' 'behind', 'inside' and 'outside' to talk about position	☺ 😐 ☹	☺ 😐 ☹
• I can use words such as 'near to', 'far from', 'around' and 'close to' to talk about position	☺ 😐 ☹	☺ 😐 ☹
• I can use words such as 'backwards', 'forwards', 'left' and 'right' to talk about direction	☺ 😐 ☹	☺ 😐 ☹
• I can talk about and make whole, half, quarter and three-quarter turns	☺ 😐 ☹	☺ 😐 ☹

	Start of the week	End of the week
• I can read and write numbers to 20 in numerals (12) and in words (twelve)	😊 😐 ☹	😊 😐 ☹
• I can order a set of numbers	😊 😐 ☹	😊 😐 ☹
• I can say the number of 10s and 1s in a number	😊 😐 ☹	😊 😐 ☹
• I can count a large set of objects	😊 😐 ☹	😊 😐 ☹
• I can count on and back in steps of 2, 5 and 10	😊 😐 ☹	😊 😐 ☹
• I can spot the missing number in a number pattern	😊 😐 ☹	😊 😐 ☹

	Start of the week	End of the week
• I can recall addition doubles to 10 + 10	😊 😐 ☹	😊 😐 ☹
• I can use doubles to work out other addition facts	😊 😐 ☹	😊 😐 ☹
• I can add together three numbers	😊 😐 ☹	😊 😐 ☹
• I know that addition can be done in any order	😊 😐 ☹	😊 😐 ☹
• I can recall addition and subtraction facts to 20	😊 😐 ☹	😊 😐 ☹
• I know how addition and subtraction facts such as 13 + 5 = 18 and 18 − 5 = 13 are related	😊 😐 ☹	😊 😐 ☹

My record sheet

Year 1
Unit 10

Name: _____

Date: _____

	Start of the week	End of the week
• I can use a ruler	😊 😐 🙁	😊 😐 🙁
• I know that 'metres' can be used to measure length	😊 😐 🙁	😊 😐 🙁
• I can estimate and measure lengths and heights	😊 😐 🙁	😊 😐 🙁
• I can solve problems involving mass	😊 😐 🙁	😊 😐 🙁

Week 1 — Multiplication and division, including Number

	Start of the week	End of the week
• I can count in steps of 2 and recognise multiples of 2	☺ 😐 ☹	☺ 😐 ☹
• I can count in steps of 5 and recognise multiples of 5	☺ 😐 ☹	☺ 😐 ☹
• I can count in steps of 10 and recognise multiples of 10	☺ 😐 ☹	☺ 😐 ☹
• I can spot the missing number in a number pattern	☺ 😐 ☹	☺ 😐 ☹
• I can use a diagram to count in groups of 2, 5 or 10	☺ 😐 ☹	☺ 😐 ☹

Week 2 — Multiplication and division

	Start of the week	End of the week
• I can count sets of 2, 5 or 10 and work out how many there are altogether	☺ 😐 ☹	☺ 😐 ☹
• I can share a group of objects into equal sets	☺ 😐 ☹	☺ 😐 ☹
• I can solve grouping and sharing problems	☺ 😐 ☹	☺ 😐 ☹

My record sheet

Year 1
Unit 11

Name: _____

Date: _____

Week 3 — 2-D and 3-D shapes

	Start of the week	End of the week
• I can spot and continue a pattern involving 2-D or 3-D shapes	😊 😐 ☹	😊 😐 ☹
• I can name common 2-D shapes in everyday objects	😊 😐 ☹	😊 😐 ☹
• I can name common 3-D shapes in everyday objects	😊 😐 ☹	😊 😐 ☹
• I can sort 2-D and 3-D shapes	😊 😐 ☹	😊 😐 ☹

	Start of the week	End of the week
• I can recall addition and subtraction facts to 20	☺ 😐 ☹	☺ 😐 ☹
• I can add and subtract one-digit and two-digit numbers	☺ 😐 ☹	☺ 😐 ☹
• I can solve addition and subtraction problems involving money	☺ 😐 ☹	☺ 😐 ☹
• I can write related addition and subtraction facts	☺ 😐 ☹	☺ 😐 ☹
• I can add 10 to a number	☺ 😐 ☹	☺ 😐 ☹
• I can subtract 10 from a number	☺ 😐 ☹	☺ 😐 ☹

	Start of the week	End of the week
• I can recall addition and subtraction facts to 20	☺ 😐 ☹	☺ 😐 ☹
• I can add a one-digit number to a two-digit number	☺ 😐 ☹	☺ 😐 ☹
• I can subtract a one-digit number from a two-digit number	☺ 😐 ☹	☺ 😐 ☹
• I can spot patterns in addition and subtraction facts	☺ 😐 ☹	☺ 😐 ☹
• I can solve missing number problems such as $16 - \Box = 9$	☺ 😐 ☹	☺ 😐 ☹
• I can solve addition and subtraction problems, writing the correct number sentence	☺ 😐 ☹	☺ 😐 ☹

My record sheet

Year 1
Unit 12

Name: _____

Date: _____

	Start of the week	End of the week
• I can read and show o'clock times	😊 😐 😞	😊 😐 😞
• I can read and show half-past times	😊 😐 😞	😊 😐 😞
• I can order o'clock and half past times	😊 😐 😞	😊 😐 😞
• I can show a time 1 hour later or 1 hour earlier than another time	😊 😐 😞	😊 😐 😞
• I can show a time half an hour later or half an hour earlier than another time	😊 😐 😞	😊 😐 😞
• I can think of things that take about 1 minute or 1 hour	😊 😐 😞	😊 😐 😞
• I can use clocks to work out how much time has passed	😊 😐 😞	😊 😐 😞

	Start of the week	End of the week
• I can find half of a shape	☺ 😐 ☹	☺ 😐 ☹
• I can find half of a set of objects	☺ 😐 ☹	☺ 😐 ☹
• I can find one quarter of a shape	☺ 😐 ☹	☺ 😐 ☹
• I can find one quarter of a set of objects	☺ 😐 ☹	☺ 😐 ☹
• I can join halves and quarters to make one whole	☺ 😐 ☹	☺ 😐 ☹
• I can show different ways of making a halve and one quarter	☺ 😐 ☹	☺ 😐 ☹
• I can use grouping and sharing to help find halves and quarters	☺ 😐 ☹	☺ 😐 ☹

Week 1 — Multiplication and division

	Start of the week	End of the week
• I can double numbers to 10	☺ 😐 ☹	☺ 😐 ☹
• I can find half of a number or a set of objects	☺ 😐 ☹	☺ 😐 ☹
• I can find one quarter of a number or a set of objects	☺ 😐 ☹	☺ 😐 ☹
• I can use grouping and sharing to help find halves and quarters	☺ 😐 ☹	☺ 😐 ☹

Year 1 Whole-class National Curriculum attainment targets

Number – Number and place value

Class: _____

Year: _____

Level of mastery key:

NYA Not yet achieved

A Achieved

A&E Achieved and exceeded

Names	count to and across 100, forwards and backwards, beginning with 0 or 1, or from any given number	count, read and write numbers to 100 in numerals; count in multiples of twos, fives and tens	given a number, identify one more and one less	identify and represent numbers using objects and pictorial representations including the number line, and use the language of: equal to, more than, less than (fewer), most, least	read and write numbers from 1 to 20 in numerals and words.	Overall level of mastery in this Domain

Number – Addition and subtraction

Class: _____

Year: _____

Level of mastery key:

NYA Not yet achieved

A Achieved

A&E Achieved and exceeded

Names	read, write and interpret mathematical statements involving addition (+), subtraction (−) and equals (=) signs	represent and use number bonds and related subtraction facts within 20	add and subtract one-digit and two-digit numbers to 20, including zero	solve one-step problems that involve addition and subtraction, using concrete objects and pictorial representations, and missing number problems such as 7 = □ − 9	Overall level of mastery in this Domain

Year 1 Whole-class National Curriculum attainment targets

Number – Multiplication and division

Class: _____

Year: _____

Level of mastery key:

NYA Not yet achieved

A Achieved

A&E Achieved and exceeded

Names	solve one-step problems involving multiplication and division, by calculating the answer using concrete objects, pictorial representations and arrays with the support of the teacher	Overall level of mastery in this Domain

Year 1 Whole-class National Curriculum attainment targets

Number – Fractions

Class: _____

Year: _____

Level of mastery key:

NYA Not yet achieved

A Achieved

A&E Achieved and exceeded

Names	recognise, find and name one half as one of two equal parts of an object, shape or quantity	recognise, find and name one quarter as one of four equal parts of an object, shape or quantity	Overall level of mastery in this Domain

© HarperCollinsPublishers Ltd. 2014

Year 1 Whole-class National Curriculum attainment targets

Measurement

Class: _____

Year: _____

Level of mastery key:

NYA Not yet achieved

A Achieved

A&E Achieved and exceeded

Names	compare, describe and solve practical problems for: – lengths and heights [for example, long/short, longer/shorter, tall/short, double/half] – mass/weight [for example, heavy/light, heavier than, lighter than] – capacity and volume [for example, full/empty, more than, less than, half, half full, quarter] – time [for example, quicker, slower, earlier, later]	measure and begin to record the following: – lengths and heights – mass/weight – capacity and volume – time (hours, minutes, seconds)	recognise and know the value of different denominations of coins and notes	sequence events in chronological order using language [for example, before and after, next, first, today, yesterday, tomorrow, morning, afternoon and evening]	recognise and use language relating to dates, including days of the week, weeks, months and years	tell the time to the hour and half past the hour and draw the hands on a clock face to show these times	Overall level of mastery in this Domain

Geometry – Properties of shapes

Class: _____

Year: _____

Level of mastery key:

NYA Not yet achieved

A Achieved

A&E Achieved and exceeded

Names	recognise and name common 2-D and 3-D shapes, including: – 2-D shapes [for example, rectangles (including squares), circles and triangles] – 3-D shapes [for example, cuboids (including cubes), pyramids and spheres]	Overall level of mastery in this Domain

Year 1 Whole-class National Curriculum attainment targets

Geometry – Position and direction

Class: _____

Year: _____

Level of mastery key:

NYA Not yet achieved

A Achieved

A&E Achieved and exceeded

Names	describe position, direction and movement, including whole, half, quarter and three-quarter turns	Overall level of mastery in this Domain

Year 1 Whole-class Domains (View 1)

Class: _____

Year: _____

Level of mastery key:

NYA Not yet achieved
A   Achieved
A&E Achieved and exceeded

Names	Year 1 National Curriculum Programme of Study Domains						
	Number – Number and place value	Number – Addition and subtraction	Number – Multiplication and division	Number – Fractions	Measurement	Geometry – Properties of shapes	Geometry – Position and direction

Class: _____ **Year:** _____

Number – Number and place value
- count to and across 100, forwards and backwards, beginning with 0 or 1, or from any given number
- count, read and write numbers to 100 in numerals; count in multiples of twos, fives and tens
- given a number, identify one more and one less
- identify and represent numbers using objects and pictorial representations including the number line, and use the language of: equal to, more than, less than (fewer), most, least
- read and write numbers from 1 to 20 in numerals and words

NYA	A	A&E

Number – Addition and subtraction
- read, write and interpret mathematical statements involving addition (+), subtraction (−) and equals (=) signs
- represent and use number bonds and related subtraction facts within 20
- add and subtract one-digit and two-digit numbers to 20, including zero
- solve one-step problems that involve addition and subtraction, using concrete objects and pictorial representations, and missing number problems such as 7 = □ − 9

NYA	A	A&E

Number – Multiplication and division
- solve one-step problems involving multiplication and division, by calculating the answer using concrete objects, pictorial representations and arrays with the support of the teacher

NYA	A	A&E

Number – Fractions
- recognise, find and name one half as one of two equal parts of an object, shape or quantity
- recognise, find and name one quarter as one of four equal parts of an object, shape or quantity

NYA	A	A&E

Measurement
- compare, describe and solve practical problems for:
  - lengths and heights [for example, long/short, longer/shorter, tall/short, double/half]
  - mass/weight [for example, heavy/light, heavier than, lighter than]
  - capacity and volume [for example, full/empty, more than, less than, half, half-full, quarter]
  - time [for example, quicker, slower, earlier, later]
- measure and begin to record the following:
  - lengths and heights
  - mass/weight
  - capacity and volume
  - time (hours, minutes, seconds)
- recognise and know the value of different denominations of coins and notes
- sequence events in chronological order using language [for example, before and after, next, first, today, yesterday, tomorrow, morning, afternoon and evening]
- recognise and use language relating to dates, including days of the week, weeks, months and years
- tell the time to the hour and half past the hour and draw the hands on a clock face to show these times

NYA	A	A&E

Geometry – Properties of shapes
- recognise and name common 2-D and 3-D shapes, including:
  - 2-D shapes [for example, rectangles (including squares), circles and triangles]
  - 3-D shapes [for example, cuboids (including cubes), pyramids and spheres]

NYA	A	A&E

Geometry – Position and direction
- describe position, direction and movement, including whole, half, quarter and three- quarter turns

NYA	A	A&E

Level of mastery key: NYA – Not yet achieved   **A** – Achieved   **A&E** – Achieved and exceeded

Year 1 Individual pupil National Curriculum attainment targets and Domains

Name: _____ Class: _____ Year: _____

Domain	National Curriculum attainment target	Level of mastery		
		Not yet achieved	Achieved	Achieved and exceeded
Number – Number and place value	Count to and across 100, forwards and backwards, beginning with 0 or 1, or from any given number			
	Count, read and write numbers to 100 in numerals; count in multiples of twos, fives and tens			
	Given a number, identify one more and one less			
	Identify and represent numbers using objects and pictorial representations including the number line, and use the language of: equal to, more than, less than (fewer), most, least			
	Read and write numbers from 1 to 20 in numerals and words.			
Number – Addition and subtraction	Read, write and interpret mathematical statements involving addition (+), subtraction (–) and equals (=) signs			
	Represent and use number bonds and related subtraction facts within 20			
	Add and subtract one-digit and two-digit numbers to 20, including zero			
	Solve one-step problems that involve addition and subtraction, using concrete objects and pictorial representations, and missing number problems such as 7 = □ – 9			
Number – Multiplication and division	Solve one-step problems involving multiplication and division, by calculating the answer using concrete objects, pictorial representations and arrays with the support of the teacher			
Number – Fractions	Recognise, find and name one half as one of two equal parts of an object, shape or quantity			
	Recognise, find and name one quarter as one of four equal parts of an object, shape or quantity			
Measurement	Compare, describe and solve practical problems for: – lengths and heights [for example, long/short, longer/shorter, tall/short, double/half] – mass/weight [for example, heavy/light, heavier than, lighter than] – capacity and volume [for example, full/empty, more than, less than, half, half full, quarter] – time [for example, quicker, slower, earlier, later]			
	Measure and begin to record the following: – lengths and heights – mass/weight – capacity and volume – time (hours, minutes, seconds)			
	Recognise and know the value of different denominations of coins and notes			

Domain	National Curriculum attainment target	Level of mastery		
		Not yet achieved	Achieved	Achieved and exceeded
Measurement	Sequence events in chronological order using language [for example, before and after, next, first, today, yesterday, tomorrow, morning, afternoon and evening]			
	Recognise and use language relating to dates, including days of the week, weeks, months and years			
	Tell the time to the hour and half past the hour and draw the hands on a clock face to show these times			
Geometry – Properties of shapes	Recognise and name common 2-D and 3-D shapes, including: – 2-D shapes [for example, rectangles (including squares), circles and triangles] – 3-D shapes [for example, cuboids (including cubes), pyramids and spheres]			
Geometry – Position and direction	Describe position, direction and movement, including whole, half, quarter and three-quarter turns			

Overall level of mastery in each of the National Curriculum Programme of Study Domains

		Level of mastery		
		Not yet achieved	Achieved	Achieved and exceeded
Domain	Number – Number and place value			
	Number – Addition and subtraction			
	Number – Multiplication and division			
	Number – Fractions			
	Measurement			
	Geometry – Properties of shapes			
	Geometry – Position and direction			

1	2	3	4
5	6	7	8
9	10	11	12
13	14	15	16
17	18	19	20

Two-digit numbers

16	19	23	28
30	37	41	42
45	54	55	57
61	64	72	79
80	86	93	98

1–100 number square

1	2	3	4	5	6	7	8	9	10
11	12	13	14	15	16	17	18	19	20
21	22	23	24	25	26	27	28	29	30
31	32	33	34	35	36	37	38	39	40
41	42	43	44	45	46	47	48	49	50
51	52	53	54	55	56	57	58	59	60
61	62	63	64	65	66	67	68	69	70
71	72	73	74	75	76	77	78	79	80
81	82	83	84	85	86	87	88	89	90
91	92	93	94	95	96	97	98	99	100

Numbers 0 to 20 in words

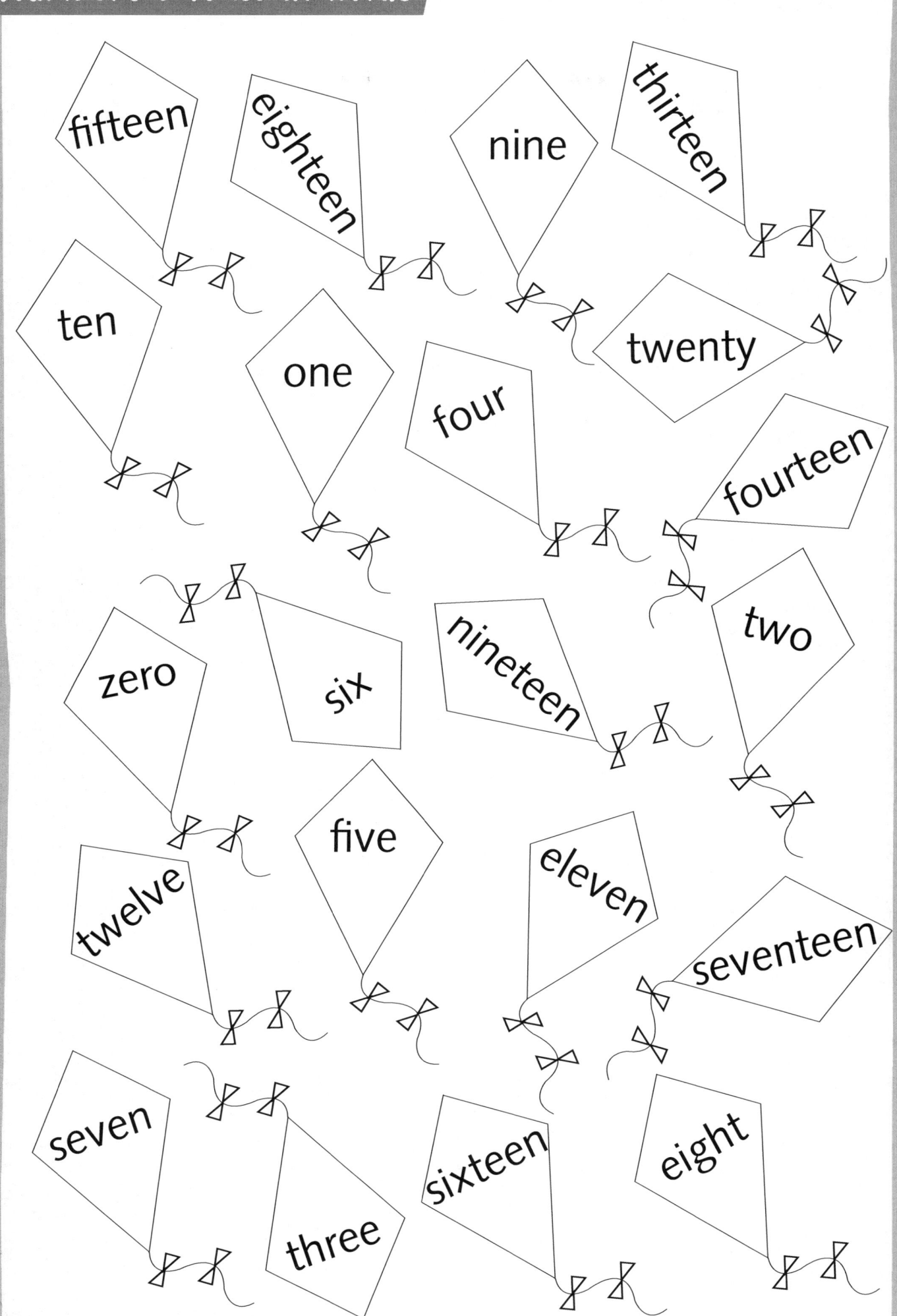

Identifying numbers

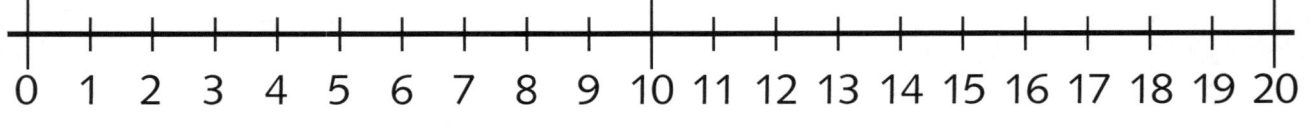

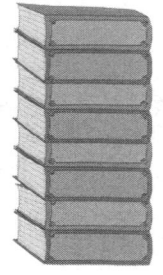

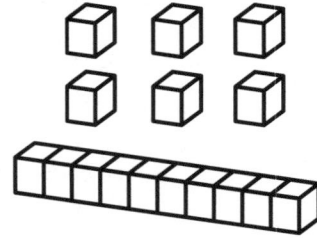

Addition number facts to 10

1 + 0 = ☐

3 + 2 = ☐

5 + 2 = ☐

2 + 2 = ☐

1 + 2 = ☐

4 + 5 = ☐

3 + 3 = ☐

8 + 2 = ☐

2 + 7 = ☐

1 + 1 = ☐

1 + 3 = ☐

6 + 2 = ☐

6 + 4 = ☐

0 + 5 = ☐

3 + 5 = ☐

3 + 4 = ☐

3 + 7 = ☐

2 + 4 = ☐

Subtraction number facts to 10

7 − 3 = ☐   5 − 2 = ☐

2 − 1 = ☐   9 − 3 = ☐

8 − 6 = ☐   3 − 2 = ☐

6 − 5 = ☐   10 − 5 = ☐

10 − 3 = ☐   1 − 1 = ☐

5 − 3 = ☐   7 − 6 = ☐

9 − 5 = ☐   10 − 6 = ☐

4 − 1 = ☐   8 − 3 = ☐

6 − 2 = ☐   4 − 2 = ☐

Addition number facts 11 to 20

9 + 6 = ☐

3 + 9 = ☐

10 + 3 = ☐

13 + 5 = ☐

15 + 4 = ☐

12 + 4 = ☐

4 + 13 = ☐

8 + 6 = ☐

7 + 4 = ☐

6 + 13 = ☐

16 + 2 = ☐

14 + 6 = ☐

7 + 13 = ☐

5 + 8 = ☐

3 + 11 = ☐

12 + 5 = ☐

5 + 11 = ☐

12 + 3 = ☐

Subtraction number facts 11 to 20

$16 - 7 = \square$

$19 - 9 = \square$

$18 - 12 = \square$

$17 - 6 = \square$

$20 - 3 = \square$

$14 - 7 = \square$

$15 - 10 = \square$

$13 - 7 = \square$

$12 - 5 = \square$

$18 - 3 = \square$

$17 - 12 = \square$

$15 - 4 = \square$

$11 - 8 = \square$

$20 - 11 = \square$

$14 - 13 = \square$

$13 - 3 = \square$

$19 - 3 = \square$

$16 - 2 = \square$

Numbers 11 to 20

Problem-solving plates

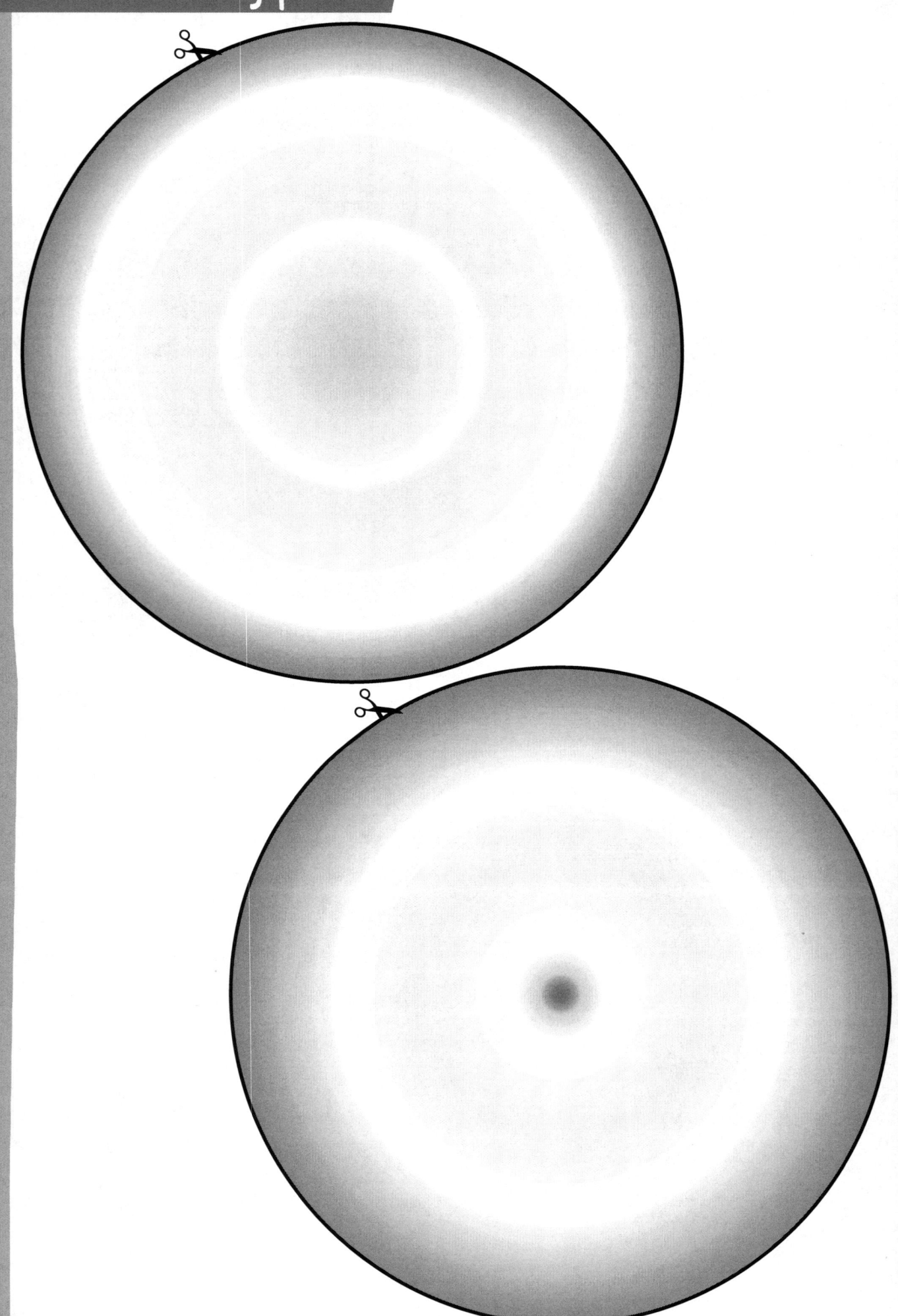

Problem-solving pictures

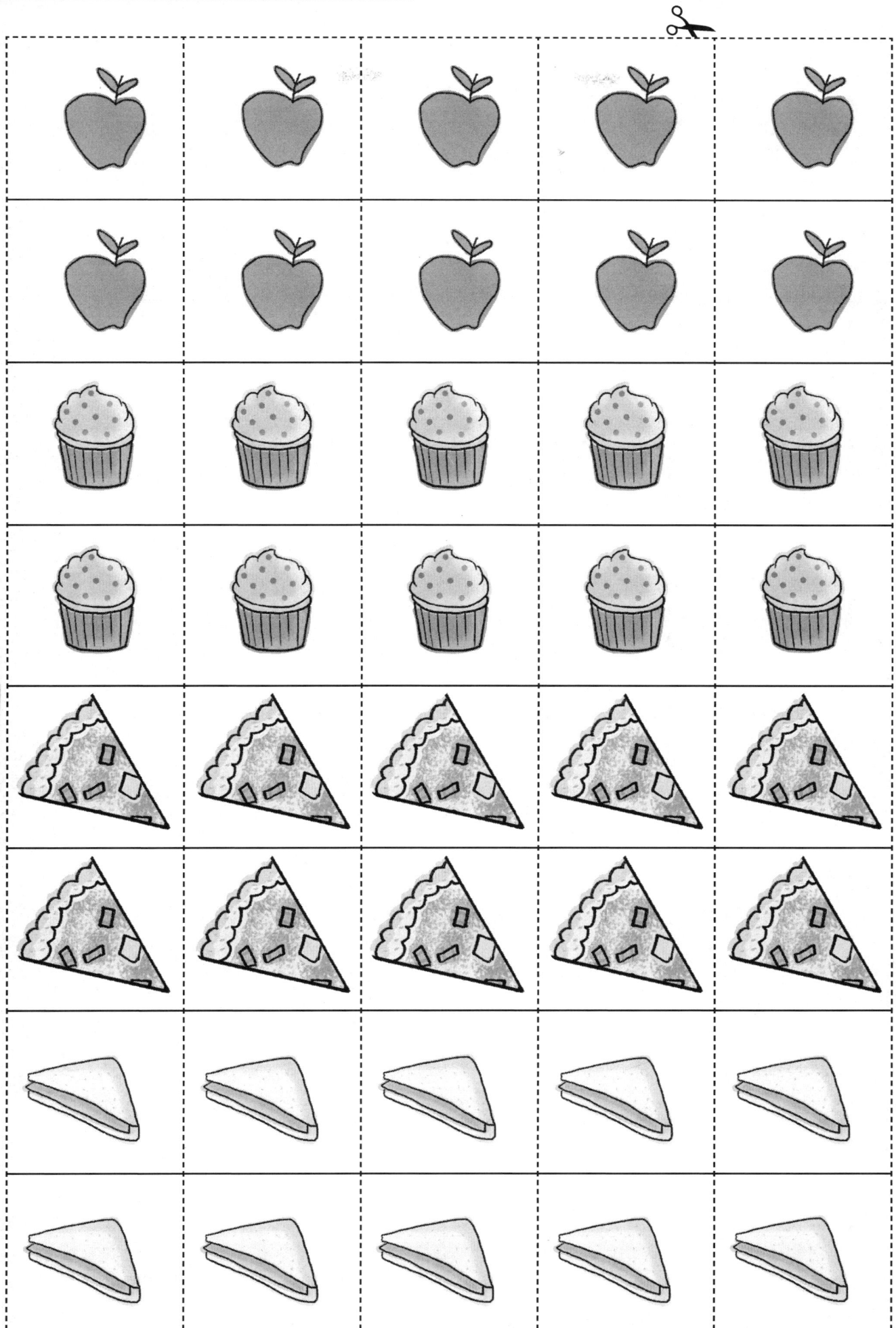

Signs and shapes cards

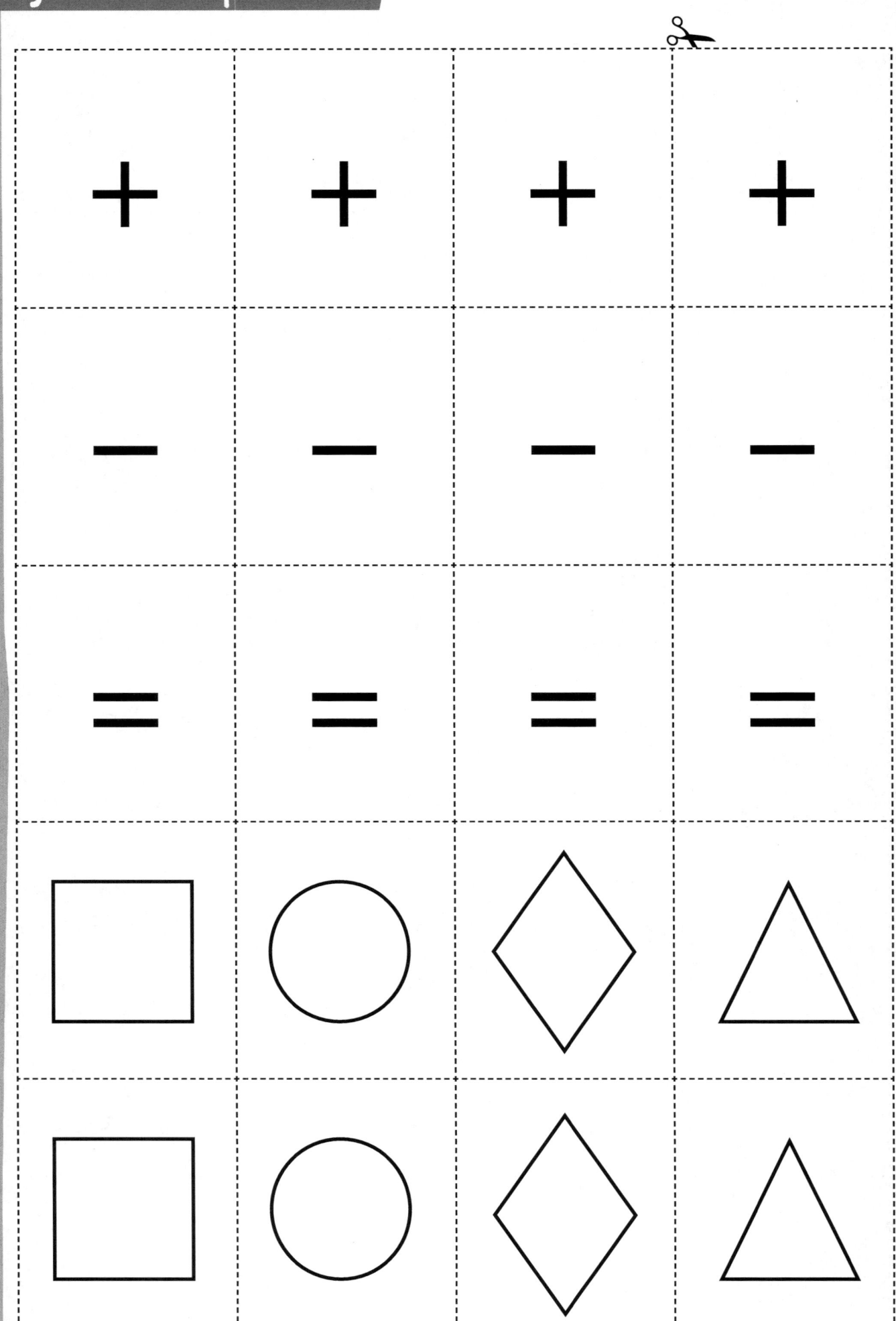

Array cards

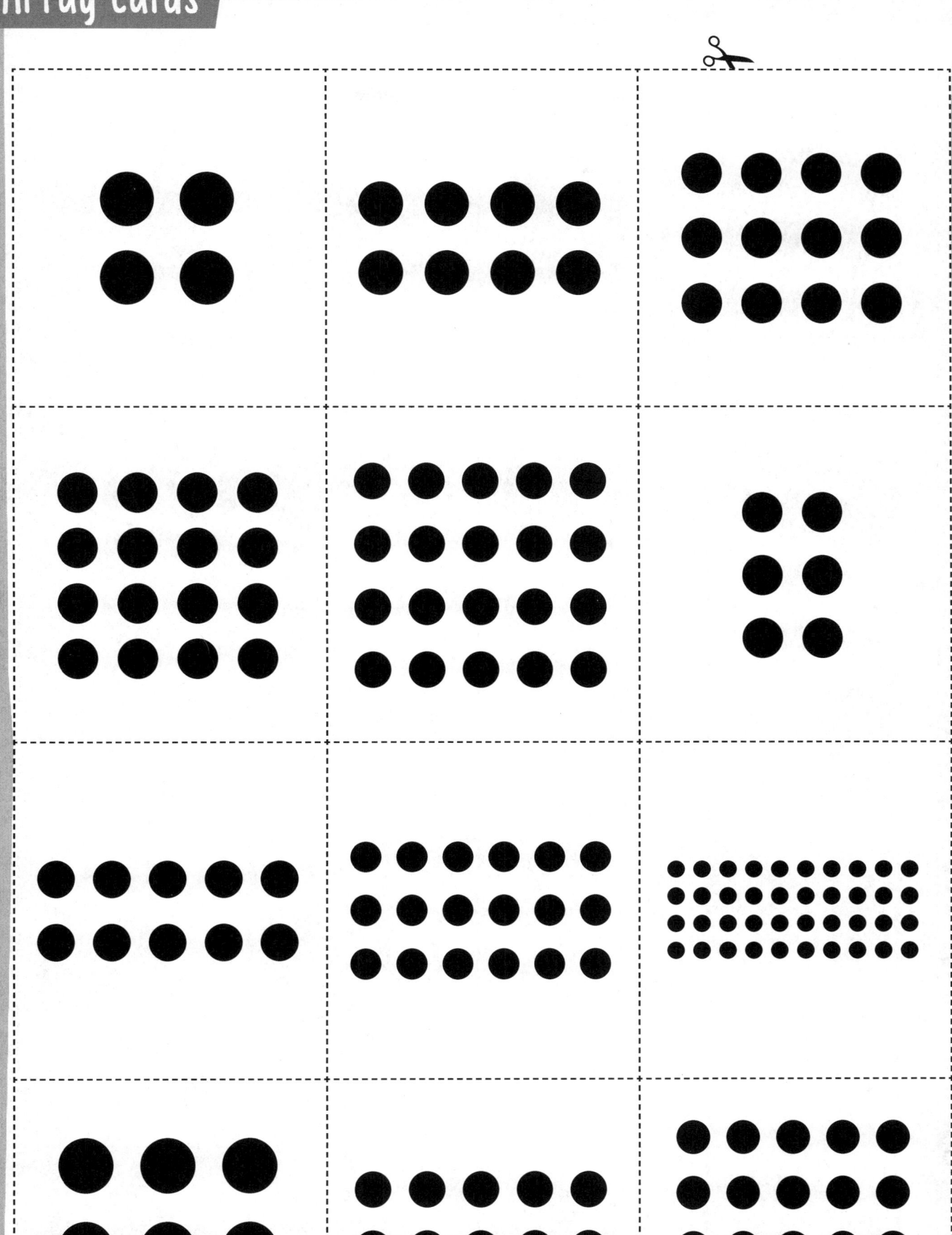

Combining groups of 2, 5 or 10

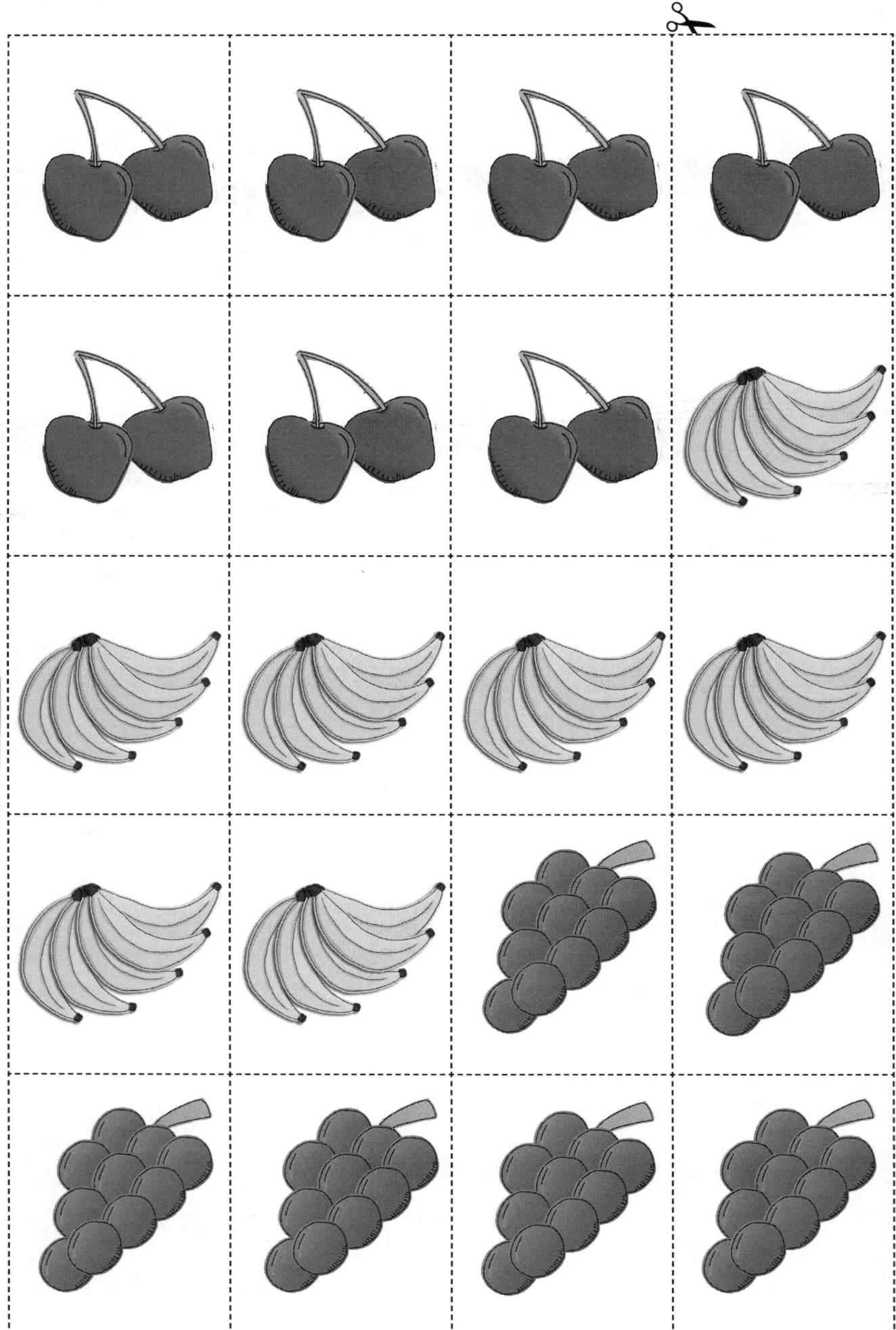

Sharing into equal groups: fields

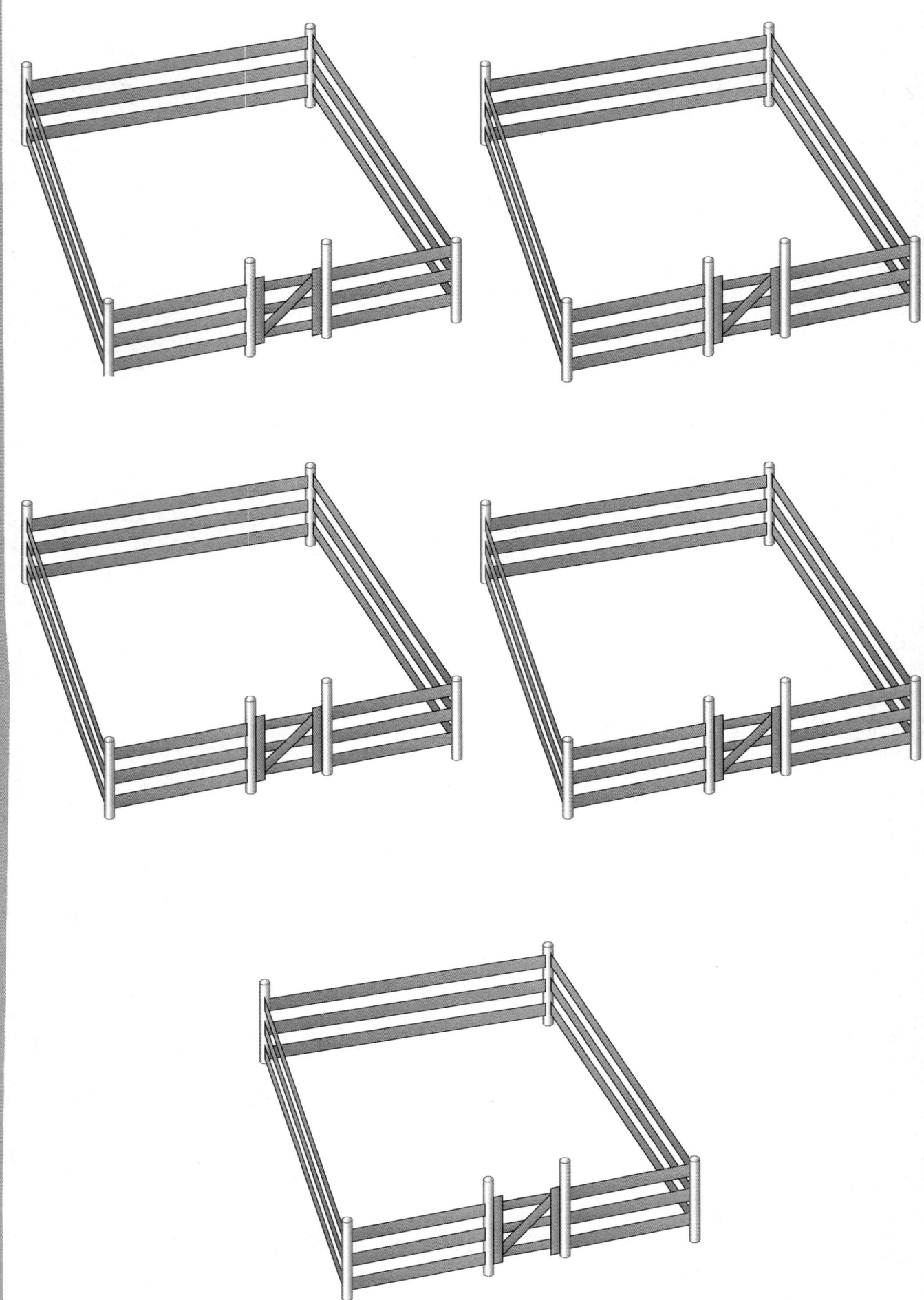

Halves and quarters (1)

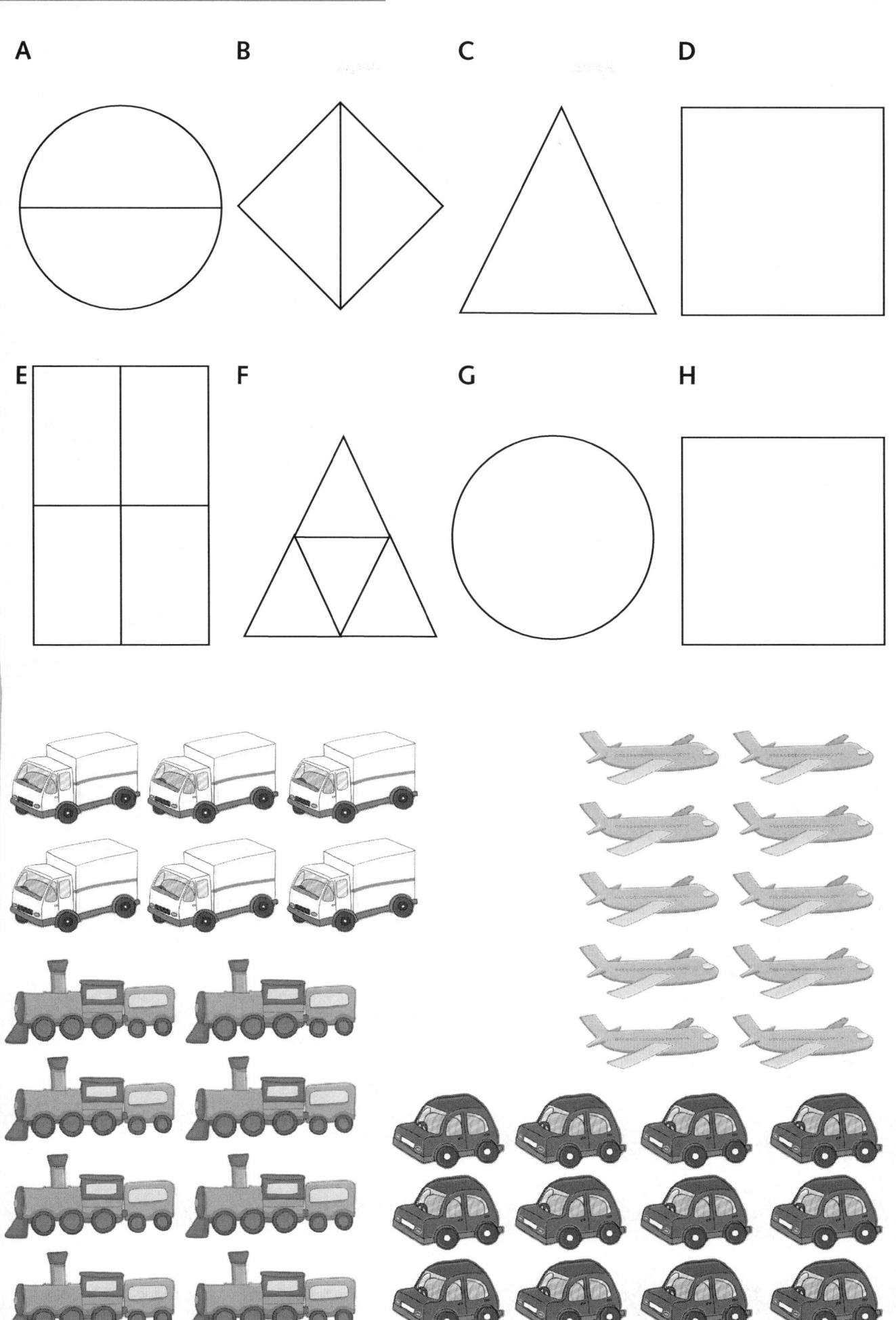

Halves and quarters (2)

Coins and notes

Sequencing events (1)

Sequencing events (2)

Monday	Tuesday	Wednesday	Thursday
Friday	Saturday	Sunday	January
Febuary	March	April	May
June	July	August	September
October	November	December	

Position and direction

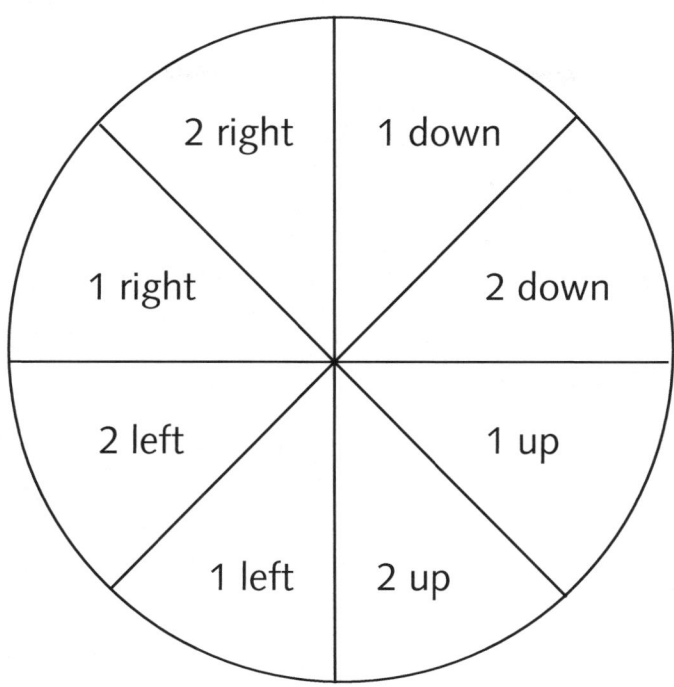

The spinner shows:

2 right	1 down
1 right	2 down
2 left	1 up
1 left	2 up

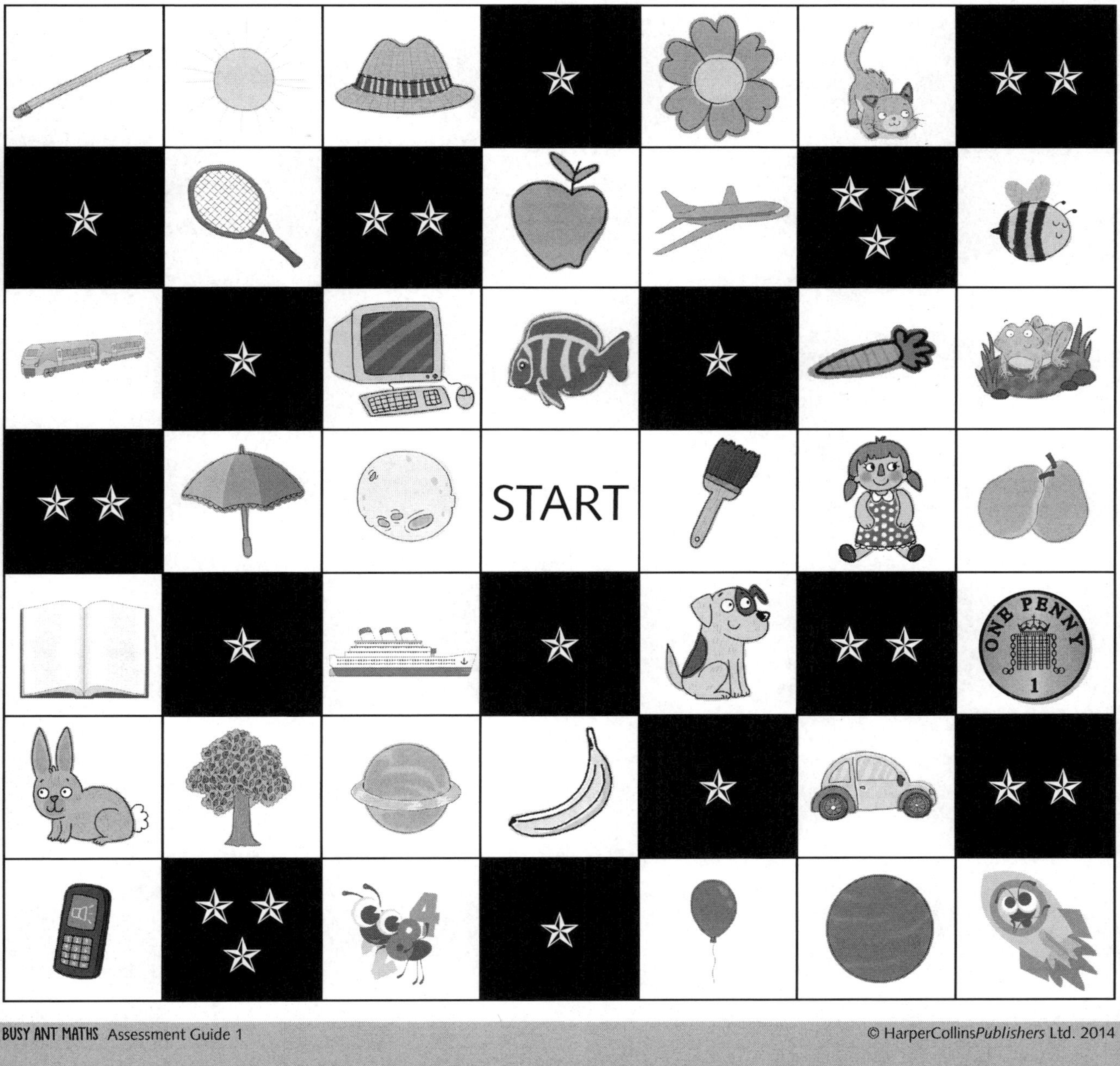

Turns

Tracking back and forward through the Mathematics National Curriculum attainment targets – Year 1

If a pupil has Not yet achieved (NYA) mastery or has Achieved and exceeded (A&E) mastery, refer to the 'Tracking back and forward through the Mathematics National Curriculum attainment targets' charts below and on pages 194–200 to determine at what year group they are currently working. Related Assessment Tasks and Assessment Exercises can be found in the corresponding Busy Ant Maths Assessment Guide.

Number – Number and place value

Early Years Outcome (40 to 60+ months) Numbers	Year 1	Year 2	Year 3	Year 4	Year 5	Year 6
Counts up to three or four objects by saying one number name for each item	count to and across 100, forwards and backwards, beginning with 0 or 1, or from any given number	count in steps of 2, 3, and 5 from 0, and in tens from any number, forward and backward	count from 0 in multiples of 4, 8, 50 and 100; find 10 or 100 more or less than a given number	count in multiples of 6, 7, 9, 25 and 1000	count forwards or backwards in steps of powers of 10 for any given number up to 1 000 000	read, write, order and compare numbers up to 10 000 000 and determine the value of each digit
Counts actions or objects which cannot be moved	count, read and write numbers to 100 in numerals; count in multiples of twos, fives and tens				read, write, order and compare numbers to 1 000 000 and determine the value of each digit	
Counts objects to 10, and beginning to count beyond 10						
Counts out up to six objects from a larger group						
Selects the correct numeral to represent 1 to 5, then 1 to 10 objects	identify and represent numbers using objects and pictorial representations including the number line, and use the language of: equal to, more than, less than (fewer), most, least	compare and order numbers from 0 up to 100; use <, > and = signs identify, represent and estimate numbers using different representations, including the number line	compare and order numbers up to 1000 identify, represent and estimate numbers using different representations	order and compare numbers beyond 1000 identify, represent and estimate numbers using different representations		
Counts an irregular arrangement of up to ten objects						
Estimates how many objects they can see and checks by counting them						
Uses the language of 'more' and 'fewer' to compare two sets of objects						
Recognises some numerals of personal significance	read and write numbers from 1 to 20 in numerals and words	read and write numbers to at least 100 in numerals and in words	read and write numbers up to 1000 in numerals and in words			
Recognises numerals 1 to 5						
Records, using marks that they can interpret and explain						
Says the number that is one more than a given number	given a number, identify one more and one less		count from 0 in multiples of 4, 8, 50 and 100; find 10 or 100 more or less than a given number	find 1000 more or less than a given number		
Finds one more or one less from a group of up to 5 objects, then 10 objects						

Early learning goal – Numbers

Children count reliably with numbers from 1 to 20, place them in order and say which number is one more or one less than a given number. Using quantities and objects, they add and subtract two single-digit numbers and count on or back to find the answer. They solve problems, including doubling, halving and sharing.

If a pupil has Not yet achieved (NYA) mastery or has Achieved and exceeded (A&E) mastery, refer to the 'Tracking back and forward through the Mathematics National Curriculum attainment targets' charts below and on page 193 and on pages 195–200 to determine at what year group they are currently working. Related Assessment Tasks and Assessment Exercises can be found in the corresponding Busy Ant Maths Assessment Guide.

Number – Addition and subtraction

Early Years Outcome (40 to 60+ months) Numbers	Year 1	Year 2	Year 3	Year 4	Year 5	Year 6
Finds the total number of items in two groups by counting all of them In practical activities and discussion, beginning to use the vocabulary involved in adding and subtracting	read, write and interpret mathematical statements involving addition (+), subtraction (–) and equals (=) signs					
	represent and use number bonds and related subtraction facts within 20	recall and use addition and subtraction facts to 20 fluently, and derive and use related facts up to 100	add and subtract numbers mentally, including: – a three-digit number and ones – a three-digit number and tens – a three-digit number and hundreds		add and subtract numbers mentally with increasingly large numbers	perform mental calculations, including with mixed operations and large numbers use their knowledge of the order of operations to carry out calculations involving the four operations
	add and subtract one-digit and two-digit numbers to 20, including zero	add and subtract numbers using concrete objects and pictorial representations, and mentally, including: – a two-digit number and ones – a two-digit number and tens – two two-digit numbers – adding three one-digit numbers				
Begins to identify own mathematical problems based on own interests and fascinations	solve one-step problems that involve addition and subtraction, using concrete objects and pictorial representations, and missing number problems such as 7 = ☐ – 9	solve problems with addition and subtraction: – using concrete objects and pictorial representations, including those involving numbers, quantities and measures – applying their increasing knowledge of mental and written methods	solve problems, including missing number problems, using number facts, place value and more complex addition and subtraction	solve addition and subtraction two-step problems in contexts, deciding which operations and methods to use and why	solve addition and subtraction multi-step problems in contexts, deciding which operations and methods to use and why	solve addition and subtraction multi-step problems in contexts, deciding which operations and methods to use and why solve problems involving addition, subtraction, multiplication and division

Early learning goal – Numbers

Children count reliably with numbers from 1 to 20, place them in order and say which number is one more or one less than a given number. Using quantities and objects, they add and subtract two single-digit numbers and count on or back to find the answer. They solve problems, including doubling, halving and sharing.

If a pupil has Not yet achieved (NYA) mastery or has Achieved and exceeded (A&E) mastery, refer to the 'Tracking back and forward' charts below and on pages 193–194 and pages 196–200 to determine at what year group they are currently working. Related Assessment Tasks and Assessment Exercises can be found in the corresponding Busy Ant Maths Assessment Guide.

Number – Multiplication and division

Early Years Outcome (40 to 60+ months) Numbers	Year 1	Year 2	Year 3	Year 4	Year 5	Year 6
	count, read and write numbers to 100 in numerals; count in multiples of twos, fives and tens [Domain: Number – Number and place value]	recall and use multiplication and division facts for the 2, 5 and 10 multiplication tables, including recognising odd and even numbers	recall and use multiplication and division facts for the 3, 4 and 8 multiplication tables	recall multiplication and division facts for multiplication tables up to 12 × 12		
Begins to identify own mathematical problems based on own interests and fascinations	solve one-step problems involving multiplication and division, by calculating the answer using concrete objects, pictorial representations and arrays with the support of the teacher	solve problems involving multiplication and division, using materials, arrays, repeated addition, mental methods and multiplication and division facts, including problems in contexts	solve problems, including missing number problems, involving multiplication and division, including positive integer scaling problems and correspondence problems in which n objects are connected to m objects	solve problems involving multiplying and adding, including using the distributive law to multiply two-digit numbers by one-digit, integer scaling problems and harder correspondence problems such as n objects are connected to m objects	solve problems involving multiplication and division including using their knowledge of factors and multiples, squares and cubes solve problems involving addition, subtraction, multiplication and division and a combination of these, including understanding the meaning of the equals sign solve problems involving multiplication and division, including scaling by simple fractions and problems involving simple rates	solve problems involving addition, subtraction, multiplication and division

Early learning goal – Numbers

Children count reliably with numbers from 1 to 20, place them in order and say which number is one more or one less than a given number. Using quantities and objects, they add and subtract two single-digit numbers and count on or back to find the answer. They solve problems, including doubling, halving and sharing.

Tracking back and forward through the Mathematics National Curriculum attainment targets – Year 1

If a pupil has Not yet achieved (NYA) mastery or has Achieved and exceeded (A&E) mastery, refer to the 'Tracking back and forward through the Mathematics National Curriculum attainment targets' charts below and on pages 193–195 and pages 197–200 to determine at what year group they are currently working. Related Assessment Tasks and Assessment Exercises can be found in the corresponding Busy Ant Maths Assessment Guide.

Early Years Outcome (40 to 60+ months) Numbers	Number – Fractions					
	Year 1	Year 2	Year 3	Year 4	Year 5	Year 6
	recognise, find and name one half as one of two equal parts of an object, shape or quantity recognise, find and name one quarter as one of four equal parts of an object, shape or quantity	recognise, find, name and write fractions $\frac{1}{3}$, $\frac{1}{4}$, $\frac{2}{4}$ and $\frac{3}{4}$ of a length, shape, set of objects or quantity write simple fractions, for example, $\frac{1}{2}$ of 6 = 3 and recognise the equivalence of $\frac{2}{4}$ and $\frac{1}{2}$	recognise, find and write fractions of a discrete set of objects: unit fractions and non-unit fractions with small denominators recognise and use fractions as numbers: unit fractions and non-unit fractions with small denominators	solve problems involving increasingly harder fractions to calculate quantities, and fractions to divide quantities, including non-unit fractions where the answer is a whole number solve simple measure and money problems involving fractions and decimals to two decimal places		

Early learning goal – Numbers

Children count reliably with numbers from 1 to 20, place them in order and say which number is one more or one less than a given number. Using quantities and objects, they add and subtract two single-digit numbers and count on or back to find the answer. They solve problems, including doubling, halving and sharing.

Tracking back and forward through the Mathematics National Curriculum attainment targets – Year 1

If a pupil has Not yet achieved (NYA) mastery or has Achieved and exceeded (A&E) mastery, refer to the 'Tracking back and forward through the Mathematics National Curriculum attainment targets' charts below and on pages 193–196 and on pages 198–200 to determine at what year group they are currently working. Related Assessment Tasks and Assessment Exercises can be found in the corresponding Busy Ant Maths Assessment Guide.

Measurement

Early Years Outcome (40 to 60+ months) Shape, space and measures	Year 1	Year 2	Year 3	Year 4	Year 5	Year 6
Orders two or three items by length or height Orders two items by weight or capacity Uses everyday language related to time Measures short periods of time in simple ways	compare, describe and solve practical problems for: – lengths and heights [for example, long/short, longer/shorter, tall/short, double/half] – mass/weight [for example, heavy/light, heavier than, lighter than] – capacity and volume [for example, full/empty, more than, less than, half, half-full, quarter] measure and begin to record the following: – lengths and heights – mass/weight – capacity and volume	compare and order lengths, mass, volume/capacity and record the results using >, < and = choose and use appropriate standard units to estimate and measure length/height in any direction (m/cm); mass (kg/g); temperature (°C); capacity (litres/ml) to the nearest appropriate unit, using rulers, scales, thermometers and measuring vessels	measure, compare, add and subtract: lengths (m/cm/mm); mass (kg/g); volume/capacity (l/ml)	estimate, compare and calculate different measures, including money in pounds and pence	use all four operations to solve problems involving measure [for example, length, mass, volume, money] using decimal notation, including scaling	solve problems involving the calculation and conversion of units of measure, using decimal notation up to three decimal places where appropriate use, read, write and convert between standard units, converting measurements of length, mass, volume and time from a smaller unit of measure to a larger unit, and vice versa, using decimal notation up to three decimal places
Beginning to use everyday language related to money	recognise and know the value of different denominations of coins and notes	recognise and use symbols for pounds (£) and pence (p); combine amounts to make a particular value find different combinations of coins that equal the same amounts of money solve simple problems in a practical context involving addition and subtraction of money of the same unit, including giving change	add and subtract amounts of money to give change, using both £ and p in practical contexts	estimate, compare and calculate different measures, including money in pounds and pence	use all four operations to solve problems involving measure [for example, length, mass, volume, money] using decimal notation, including scaling	solve problems involving the calculation and conversion of units of measure, using decimal notation up to three decimal places where appropriate

If a pupil has Not yet achieved (NYA) mastery or has Achieved and exceeded (A&E) mastery, refer to the 'Tracking back and forward through the Mathematics National Curriculum attainment targets' charts below and on pages 193–197 and pages 199–200 to determine at what year group they are currently working. Related Assessment Tasks and Assessment Exercises can be found in the corresponding Busy Ant Maths Assessment Guide.

Measurement Continued

Early Years Outcome (40 to 60+ months) Shape, space and measures	Year 1	Year 2	Year 3	Year 4	Year 5	Year 6
Orders and sequences familiar events	sequence events in chronological order using language [for example, before and after, next, first, today, yesterday, tomorrow, morning, afternoon and evening]	compare and sequence intervals of time	compare durations of events [for example to calculate the time taken by particular events or tasks]			
	compare, describe and solve practical problems for: – time [for example, quicker, slower, earlier, later] measure and begin to record the following: – time (hours, minutes, seconds) recognise and use language relating to dates, including days of the week, weeks, months and years	know the number of minutes in an hour and the number of hours in a day	know the number of seconds in a minute and the number of days in each month, year and leap year estimate and read time with increasing accuracy to the nearest minute; record and compare time in terms of seconds, minutes and hours; use vocabulary such as o'clock, a.m./p.m., morning, afternoon, noon and midnight	convert between different units of measure [for example, kilometre to metre; hour to minute] solve problems involving converting from hours to minutes; minutes to seconds; years to months; weeks to days	solve problems involving converting between units of time	use, read, write and convert between standard units, converting measurements of length, mass, volume and time from a smaller unit of measure to a larger unit, and vice versa, using decimal notation up to three decimal places
	tell the time to the hour and half past the hour and draw the hands on a clock face to show these times	tell and write the time to five minutes, including quarter past/to the hour and draw the hands on a clock face to show these times	tell and write the time from an analogue clock, including using Roman numerals from I to XII, and 12-hour and 24-hour clocks	read, write and convert time between analogue and digital 12- and 24-hour clocks		

Early learning goal – shape, space and measures

Children use everyday language to talk about size, weight, capacity, position, distance, time and money to compare quantities and objects and to solve problems. They recognise, create and describe patterns. They explore characteristics of everyday objects and shapes and use mathematical language to describe them.

Tracking back and forward through the Mathematics National Curriculum attainment targets – Year 1

If a pupil has Not yet achieved (NYA) mastery or has Achieved and exceeded (A&E) mastery, refer to the 'Tracking back and forward through the Mathematics National Curriculum attainment targets' charts below and on pages 193–198 and page 200 to determine at what year group they are currently working. Related Assessment Tasks and Assessment Exercises can be found in the corresponding Busy Ant Maths Assessment Guide.

Geometry – Properties of shapes

Early Years Outcome (40 to 60+ months) Shape, space and measures	Year 1	Year 2	Year 3	Year 4	Year 5	Year 6
Beginning to use mathematical names for 'solid' 3-D shapes and 'flat' 2-D shapes, and mathematical terms to describe shapes Selects a particular named shape Uses familiar objects and common shapes to create and recreate patterns and build models	recognise and name common 2-D and 3-D shapes, including: – 2-D shapes, and 'flat' 2-D shapes, and mathematical terms [for example, rectangles (including squares), circles and triangles]	compare and sort common 2-D and 3-D shapes and everyday objects identify and describe the properties of 2-D shapes, including the number of sides and line symmetry in a vertical line	draw 2-D shapes and make 3-D shapes using modelling materials; recognise 3-D shapes in different orientations and describe them	compare and classify geometric shapes, including quadrilaterals and triangles, based on their properties and sizes identify lines of symmetry in 2-D shapes presented in different orientations complete a simple symmetric figure with respect to a specific line of symmetry	use the properties of rectangles to deduce related facts and find missing lengths and angles distinguish between regular and irregular polygons based on reasoning about equal sides and angles	draw 2-D shapes using given dimensions and angles compare and classify geometric shapes based on their properties and sizes and find unknown angles in any triangles, quadrilaterals, and regular polygons illustrate and name parts of circles, including radius, diameter and circumference and know that the diameter is twice the radius
Beginning to use mathematical names for 'solid' 3-D shapes and 'flat' 2-D shapes, and mathematical terms to describe shapes Selects a particular named shape Uses familiar objects and common shapes to create and recreate patterns and build models	recognise and name common 2-D and 3-D shapes, including: – 3-D shapes [for example, cuboids (including cubes), pyramids and spheres]	compare and sort common 2-D and 3-D shapes and everyday objects identify and describe the properties of 3-D shapes, including the number of edges, vertices and faces identify 2-D shapes on the surface of 3-D shapes, [for example, a circle on a cylinder and a triangle on a pyramid]	draw 2-D shapes and make 3-D shapes using modelling materials; recognise 3-D shapes in different orientations and describe them		identify 3-D shapes, including cubes and other cuboids, from 2-D representations	compare and classify geometric shapes based on their properties and sizes and find unknown angles in any triangles, quadrilaterals, and regular polygons recognise, describe and build simple 3-D shapes, including making nets

Early learning goal – shape, space and measures

Children use everyday language to talk about size, weight, capacity, position, distance, time and money to compare quantities and objects and to solve problems. They recognise, create and describe patterns. They explore characteristics of everyday objects and shapes and use mathematical language to describe them.

Tracking back and forward through the Mathematics National Curriculum attainment targets – Year 1

If a pupil has Not yet achieved (NYA) mastery or has Achieved and exceeded (A&E) mastery, refer to the 'Tracking back and forward through the Mathematics National Curriculum attainment targets' charts below and on pages 193–199 to determine at what year group they are currently working. Related Assessment Tasks and Assessment Exercises can be found in the corresponding Busy Ant Maths Assessment Guide.

Geometry – Position and direction

Early Years Outcome (40 to 60+ months) Shape, space and measures	Year 1	Year 2	Year 3	Year 4	Year 5	Year 6
Can describe their relative position such as 'behind' or 'next to'	describe position, direction and movement, including whole, half, quarter and three-quarter turns	use mathematical vocabulary to describe position, direction and movement, including movement in a straight line and distinguishing between rotation as a turn and in terms of right angles for quarter, half and three-quarter turns (clockwise and anti-clockwise)	recognise angles as a property of shape or a description of a turn [Domain: Geometry – Properties of shapes] identify right angles, recognise that two right angles make one half-turn, three make three quarters of a turn and four a complete turn; identify whether angles are greater than or less than a right angle [Domain: Geometry – Properties of shapes]			